The Cultural Politics of Heiner Müller

The Cultural Politics of Heiner Müller

Edited by

Dan Friedman

Cambridge Scholars Publishing

The Cultural Politics of Heiner Müller, Edited by Dan Friedman

This book first published 2007 by

Cambridge Scholars Publishing

15 Angerton Gardens, Newcastle, NE5 2JA, UK

British Library Cataloguing in Publication Data
A catalogue record for this book is available from the British Library

ISBN (10): 1-84718-396-4, ISBN (13): 9781847183965

TABLE OF CONTENTS

Part III
Waiting for History: Müller and the Dynamics of Culture and Politics in the 21st Century

INTRODUCTION

THE CULTURAL POLITICS OF HEINER MÜLLER

1.

The origins of this collection go back to 1987 when Eva Brenner, then a graduate student in performance studies at New York University, convinced her colleagues at the Castillo Theatre in New York City (including me) to stage Heiner Müller's *Explosion of a Memory/Description of a Picture*. She invited her friend Joseph Szeiler, then artistic director of the Angelus Novus theater in her native Vienna, to fly to New York and direct the production.

The Castillo Theatre in 1987 was three years old. It consisted of a contentious collection of community organizers, leftist political activists and artists trying to work together (not easy with such an opinionated bunch) to build a theatre with ties to New York's poor and working class communities. Some of us came out of the street theatres of the late 1960s and '70s, others out of the feminist oriented stand-up comedy scene. Still other Castillo founders, not originally theatre people at all, but figurative painters, modern dancers, and musicians, looked for new political art to emerge from the street, from the then coming-into-being hip-hop culture (graffiti, rap, break-dancing and so on). It will come as no surprise then that not all of us were thrilled about producing a seemingly impenetrable dramatic poem by a German avant-gardist who appeared to have little to say to the communities we were organizing.

Fred Newman is a former philosophy professor who had left academia in 1968 to become a community organizer. By 1987 he was the leader of the political movement/community that Brenner, myself, and the rest of the Castillo founders were a part of. He was of the opinion that it was Castillo's obligation to bring the poor and working class people we were organizing into contact with the work of the most challenging and experimental artists. It is ordinary people, he argued, who had the most to gain from getting past traditional ways of seeing and they who, in the long run, had the power to do something with the experiences that Müller's texts could provide.

Newman and Brenner won the rest of us over. Castillo produced *Explosion of a Memory/Description of a Picture* and brought out hundreds of community people to see it. In the years since that first production, Castillo has mounted 15 Müller productions—including the North American premier of *The Task* in 1989 and of *Germania 3 Ghosts at Dead Man* in 2002—most of them directed by Newman, who was Castillo's artistic director from 1989 until his retirement in December 2005.

Over the course of this work, Castillo and Müller built a relationship. In 1989, Müller visited Castillo and met with Newman; that same year, Castillo artists, including Brenner, visited him in Berlin. Thereafter, Castillo sent videos of its Müller productions to the playwright. For Castillo's 1992 production of *Explosion* (this one under Newman's direction) Müller contributed a video of himself reading the text in English from a Berlin rooftop. He was scheduled to lead a two-week workshop with Castillo's actors in February 1996, but passed away before that was possible. His protégé, Stephan Suschke, came in his stead in 1996 to see Newman's all-female production of *Hamletmachine* and returned the following year to direct *Despoiled Shore Medeamaterial Landscape with Argonauts* at Castillo.

In the late 1990s we decided that producing Müller at Castillo was not enough. We came to feel his work was so significant—all the more so in the post-communist world—that we wanted to play an active role in generating dialogue about Müller and encouraging others to produce his work. Castillo's efforts in this regard have included organizing public dialogues about Müller between Newman and others who had directed and/or studied his work. Participants in these forums over the years have included: Sylvère Lotringer, editor of *Germania*, an invaluable collection of Müller interviews (cited often by contributors to this volume); Jonathan Kalb, author of *The Theater of Heiner Müller*; Stephan Suschke, who had worked as Müller's dramaturg and assistant director, first at the Deutsches Theater and later at the Berliner Ensemble; and a number of other innovative Müller directors from around the U.S. The largest of these discussions was between Newman and Robert Wilson in February 2002. It took place before a full house of 600 theater artists, students and community organizers at John Jay College of the City University of New York.[1] Castillo also publishes a journal, *Müller in America,* to promote the study of Müller and his work.[2] In April of 2005, Castillo organized a conference on "The Cultural Politics of Heiner Müller," at the Castillo Theatre's then new facility on 42nd Street near Times Square in New York City.[3]

The articles in this collection grow out of that conference. The gathering attracted artists and scholars from across the United States, Canada and France. In addition to the papers delivered (versions of which make up this book), artists in attendance came from Castillo as well as from the DNA Theatre in Toronto and Scènes theâtre cinéma in Lyons, France (the only theatre in the world that, according to Carl Weber, has produced more Müller than Castillo). Regular Castillo theater-goers attended as well, many of them having spent over a decade wrestling, as we did, with the work of Müller.

In fact, the conference's opening panel was entitled "An Audience for Heiner Müller." It was moderated by Castillo's managing director Diane Stiles and brought together six audience members to discuss their reactions to and thoughts about the Müller work they have experienced at Castillo. The panel put the difficulty of Müller's texts front and center, raised the issue of accessibility and created a context for the conversations that continued all weekend.

The conference began on Friday night with a reception followed by a performance of *Medeamaterial/Landscape With Argonauts* by students from Mount Allison University (New Brunswick, Canada) under the direction of Cordula Quint. On Saturday night, many conference participants attended the Castillo production of *Revising Germany* by Newman under the direction of Gabrielle L. Kurlander, a play that includes both Brecht and Müller as characters. Both Castillo and Scènes theâtre cinéma gave reports, which included video segments, on their theatres' Müller production histories, and Philippe Vincent, Scènes artistic director, performed the entire "Man in the Elevator" speech from *The Task* in French.

Each chapter of this book, while based on a paper delivered at the conference, has gone through substantial expansion and deepening. Not everyone who presented at the conference is included; some could not subsequently be located and a few opted out of the project. At the same time, I have included contributions from three artist-scholars—Eva Brenner, Aleksander Sasha Lukac, and Carl Weber—who were unable to attend the conference, but were eager to contribute to the project. I felt passionately that they each had important things to say about the cultural politics of Heiner Müller.

This book is, therefore, not, strictly speaking, a transcript of the conference. It is at once an outgrowth, a further development, and an extension of the initial gathering, an event that, thanks to Cambridge Scholars Publishing, will now reach a far wider audience than those who came together to talk about Heiner Müller on that April weekend.

2.

Who Heiner Müller is and the cultural and political significance of his work will be discussed in some detail in the pages that follow. For those meeting Müller (1929-1995) for the first time, he was a life-long Marxist and experimental playwright who spent his adult life in the German Democratic Republic (GDR). He is probably the most theatrically and politically challenging playwright of our epoch.

Starting as a protégé of Bertolt Brecht, Müller evolved into one of the great innovative poets of the 20th Century, writing texts for the stage that seem to defy the limitations of the theater. Not only do his later texts have no plot, they are often devoid of specific characters and even dialogue. "Only when a text cannot be done in the theatre as it is now," Müller remarked in 1975, "can it be productive for the theatre, or interesting." (Müller, 1975: 120) Müller considered his texts simply starting points for creation. "What bores me in the productions [of my plays] is that they [the directors] simply illustrate what is already in the text, instead of using it as association material, as a kind of supernova which inspires directors with ideas." (Müller, 1990: 211)

Müller is also the most politically sophisticated and provocative of Europe's post-World War II playwrights. He was a communist whose work was banned for years by the Communist government of the GDR. Müller offended the bureaucrats and political thugs who ran East Germany with his brutal, beautiful and honest dissection of the culture and politics of Eastern Europe. At the same time, Müller infuriated (or at least annoyed) the anti-communists and liberals of the West because he refused to leave the GDR or become a "dissident." As deformed as it was, the communist experiment—"the petrification of a hope," as he called it in his play *Hamletmachine* (Müller, 1984: 56)—was, for Müller, the only chance for a better world that history offered in the 20th Century.

Because he came out on the losing side of the Cold War, Müller has been dismissed by some as an historical and political anachronism. For others, his challenges to theatrical convention and the ideological assumptions inherent in those conventions, as well the content of his theater texts—that wrestle with, among many other things, issues of women's oppression, terrorism and the inherent power of the impoverished peoples of the South—point toward the future. Whatever political and/or aesthetic judgment one brings to Müller's work, it is clear that in many ways he is a transitional figure, artistically bridging modernism and postmodernism, and politically linking the East-West divisions of the Cold War with the North-South confrontations that have come to the fore in the post-communist world. Müller is also the only major artist produced by the 20th Century communist movement to live through its collapse and to examine the implications of its demise, including the subsequent rise of international terrorism. Like his mentor Brecht, Müller's dramaturgy and politics are inextricably interwoven.

All of this makes him a figure of increasing interest not only to theater artists and scholars, but also to students of literature and politics, to historians, political scientists, sociologists, psychologists—and all those concerned with the intersection of culture and politics, an intersection that has become increasingly congested in our post-communist, post-modern, post-9/11 world. Hence our title: "Cultural Politics." While not a precise term, cultural politics has the advantage of implying/generating an exploration of what is *cultural* about politics and what is *political* about culture. It is the working assumption of the contributors to this collection that the cultural and political are inseparable when examining Müller's work and influence.

3.

The topics explored in this collection are very narrow and very broad. Narrow in the sense that they are all about Heiner Müller and his work in the theatre. Broad in that Heiner Müller's life and work assimilated/embodied/played with/transformed the legacy of German and European theatre and literature, German and international communist history, Western philosophy and political thought. His erudition was vast—a deep well from which he drew continually. A single page of text in his play *Hamletmachine*, for example, includes dozens of allusions, quotations, paraphrases and literary and historical references. However, for our authors, the extent of Müller's knowledge is not the point. What he did with this legacy—to build on it, to create anew with it—is.

While each of the chapters in this book focuses on a specific aspect of Müller's cultural politics, they share a number overlapping concerns. Virtually all of them look at Müller in relation to German, communist and world history, and most of them see an organic link between that history and the content and form of his work. Many of the chapters touch on Müller's political and cultural relationship with his mentor Bertolt Brecht, although they don't always agree on the nature of that relationship. A third thread running through the essays is an exploration of Müller's relationship to and role in shaping postmodernism in the theater. Obviously, that exploration is related to his relationship with Brecht, but it goes beyond the specifics of that bond to Müller's attitude(s) toward the modernist ideology of Marxism, or perhaps more to the point, to ideology itself as a modernist construct and concern. While our authors come at this question from different angles, many see in Müller's radical re-visioning of dramatic structure a challenge to the ideological assumptions of modernism.

Despite these overlapping concerns, I have chosen to organize the essays into three sections, each focusing on what I see as a distinct area of Müller's cultural politics. The first section, "The Frozen Storm: Müller and the Realpolitik of the Cold War," contains essays exploring Müller's political attitudes and practices within the specific context of the Cold War in which he lived much of his creative life. The second, "Digging Up the Dead: Müller's Use and Transformation of the Western Tradition," looks at how and why Müller built on the forms, images, characters and plays of the Western cultural tradition in an attempt to re-create and reshape it. The third section, "Waiting for History: Müller and the Dynamics of Culture and Politics in the 21st Century," looks, from a number of (sometimes conflicting) perspectives, at the implications of Müller's work for the unfolding political and cultural dynamics of the new century. These categories will, I hope, prove to be of some value to the reader. I have attempted to explain (rationalize?) that value in a brief introduction to each section.

This slim volume, like the modest conference that gave it birth, makes no claim to completeness. What I think it does offer are some very interesting and provocative essays that I hope will lead to further interest in and discussion of Heiner Müller and his work.

Dan Friedman
Castillo Theatre
New York City
September 2007

Notes

[1] The transcript of that conversation, "Robert Wilson and Fred Newman: A Dialogue on Politics and Therapy, Stillness and Vaudeville" moderated by Richard Schechner was published in *The Drama Review* in the Fall of 2003, T179: 113-128. A video of the dialogue can be ordered from the Castillo Theatre, boxoffice@allstars.org.

[2] Volume 1 of *Müller in America* is a collection articles by American and Canadian directors about their productions of Müller texts. It includes a Foreword by Carl Weber and articles by: Sue-Ellen Case, Jeff Burke, Charles Duncombe, Steve Earnest and Joel Elis, Babak Ebrahimian, Keith Fowler, Nick Fracaro, Aleksandar

Sahsa Lukac, Scott Magelssen and John Troyer, Joe Martin, Fred Newman, Cordula Quint, James Slowiak, Stephan Sushke, and Robert Wilson.
[3] A report on the conference can be found in: Friedman, Dan. "Heiner Müller on 42nd Street," The Literary Managers and Dramaturgs of the Americas, *Review*, Vol. 15, Issue 2 (Spring/Summer 2005): 7-8.

Work Cited

Müller, Heiner (1975). "Der Dramatiker und die Geschichte seiner Zeit. Ein Gesprach zwischen Horst Laube und Heiner Müller." *Theater Heute*, Sonderhelft: 119-207. Translation by Eva Brenner, quoted in "HAMLETMACHINE Onstage: A Critical Analysis of Heiner Müller's Play in Production." (1993). Dissertation. New York University: 76.

—. (1984). *Hamletmachine and Other Texts for the Stage*. In Carl Weber (Trans.). New York: Performing Arts Journal Publications.

—. (1990). *Germania*, Ed. Sylvère Lotringer. Trans. Bernard and Caroline Schütze. New York: Semiotext(e), 1990.

PART I

THE FROZEN STORM:
MÜLLER AND THE REALPOLITIK
OF THE COLD WAR

I, my grave his face, I: the woman with the wound at her throat, right and left in her hands the split bird, blood on the mouth, I: the bird who with the script of his beak shows the murderer the way into the night, I: the frozen storm.
—Heiner Müller, 1984

INTRODUCTION

Heiner Müller, like us all, was a product of his time and place. The chapters in section one look at Müller and the art he created in the context of that time and place and examine the ways in which his life and theatre responded to and impacted on the history he was a part of. Time and place are expansive words that can be approached from many angles and which yield many shades of meaning.

Carl Weber, Müller's major English translator, provides us with a brief political biography of the playwright. Having been a close colleague and friend of Müller's and having developed as an artist in the same cultural and political milieu, Weber is particularly well situated to provide this overview. Slightly older than Müller, Weber joined the Berliner Ensemble in 1952 as an actor, dramaturg and assistant director to Bertolt Brecht, with whom he worked on the productions of *Katzgraben*, *Caucasian Chalk Circle*, and *Galileo*. After Brecht's death in 1956, Weber became one of the company's directors, staging *Mother Courage* and *Fear and Misery in the Third Reich,* and acting in eight other Ensemble productions. Since leaving the East in 1961, he has directed in numerous theatres in Western Europe and the United States. In 1966 he was a founding member of the faculty of the now world-renowned New York University Tisch School of the Arts. Since 1984, he has been professor of dramaturgy and directing at Stanford; it is from Stanford that he has translated the bulk of Müller's dramatic work into English.

In "From Determination to Detachment—Heiner Müller's Assessment of Culture and Politics in a Lifetime of Profound Historical Change," Weber traces Müller's political evolution from the social democratic politics of his father (which resulted in his father's internment in a Nazi concentration camp) through the playwright's response to the collapse of the Soviet model of socialism six years before his death. It is a journey, Weber, points out, that "never ceased to be marked by the visceral experience of German fascism." By tracing the specifics of Müller's "straddling" of the twists and turns of the Cold War, Weber makes clear that Müller was *the* political dramatist of that period of political and ideological stalemate and stagnation, the "frozen storm" referred to in *Explosion of a Memory/ Description of a Picture.*

Aleksandar Sasha Lukac, a generation younger than Müller and Weber, brings to "The Dissident's Dilemma: Müller's Choice to Stay in East Germany," not a friendship with the playwright, but a set of somewhat parallel experiences and concerns. Lukac, the former artistic director of the National Theatre in Belgrade and the independent political theatre Plexus Boris Piljnjak, has been living in Toronto, Canada for some 15 years. Like Müller, he grew to artistic maturity facing the painful contradictions of a progressive artist working within the repressive, yet nominally socialist Eastern Bloc. While making clear and important distinctions between the political cultures of the former Yugoslavia and the German Democratic Republic, Lukac none-the-less draws on his own experiences to explore not only why Müller chose to stay in the GDR, but why that decision was essential to the theatre that he created.

Eva Brenner, who contributes the third chapter to this section, is a pioneer of Müller scholarship. (That her 1993 dissertation, "HAMLETMACHINE Onstage: A Critical Analysis of Heiner Müller's Play in Production," is cited by half our contributors is evidence of her influence.) In her essay, "A Cancer Walk Through German History," Brenner broadens the lens considerably on Müller's time and place. She considers Müller in the context of German history stretching back to the 17th Century and looks at Germany not primarily as a geographical location but as the epicenter of 20th Century history. Building on Walter Benjamin's non-schematic and open-ended concept of history, she looks at Müller's work as a response to the failures of German history, in particular to the failure of the aborted German Communist Revolution of 1919. In so doing, she not only (or even primarily) sheds new light on Müller's relationship to/treatment of German history, but also makes a persuasive case for locating Müller's universal appeal in his German-ness.

Each of the contributors to this section has taken a different approach to examining Müller's engagement with the real politics of his time and place and with the impact of that engagement on his work. They have hardly exhausted the subject, but taken together these chapters function as a helpful springboard into the rest of our book.

Work Cited

Müller, Heiner (1989). *Explosion of a Memory*. Ed and trans. Carl Weber. New York: Performing Arts Journal Publications: 102.

CHAPTER ONE

FROM DETERMINATION TO DETACHMENT—
HEINER MÜLLER'S ASSESSMENT OF CULTURE
AND POLITICS IN A LIFETIME OF PROFOUND
HISTORICAL CHANGE

CARL WEBER

It might be perceived as not too difficult to construe a somewhat coherent, if at times conflicted, progress of the cultural politics or, perhaps more acurrately, the cultural and political positions, Heiner Müller espoused during his career as a writer and also, eventually, a sought-after popular commentator. However, it turns out to be a complicated endeavor, since Müller's view of cultural (and other) politics kept changing, often drastically changing, throughout his life. Sometimes these changes evolved in a slow and considered manner. Every so often they were a spontaneous response to the historical moment and its implications—as well to personal experiences connected to, but not necessarily elicited by, historical incident.

Heiner Müller moved during his lifetime from a firmly committed ideological position to a rather distanced view of ideologies and history, "the view of an archaeologist of history," as his friend, the scholar Hans Thies Lehmann has noted (Lehmann/Primavesi: 12). In fact, reviewing the numerous statements Müller formulated during a life that kept "straddling," as he liked to call it, the divide which marked world culture during half a century of Cold Warfare, one recognizes an often conflicted, yet nevertheless distinct, passage from the narrowly defined positions he adopted in the 1950s, i.e. in his twenties, to a much broader and decidedly more pessimistic view of the cultural and political currents he discerned in the past and future of the human race. However, throughout his life he fundamentally concurred with a Marxist interpretation of history and the concomitant hope for the ultimate establishment of a society that would abolish the vast gap between the haves and the have-nots which has characterized all of human history or, as he preferred to label it, (following Marx) prehistory (Müller/Weber 1989b, 106).

Müller's worldview and writings never ceased to be marked by the visceral experience of German fascism. In the period of the Nazis' rise to power his father was a functionary of the Socialist Workers Party, a political group that had split from the Social Democrats and moved closer to the Communist Party; it was one among several left parties active during the later years of the Weimar Republic. He was arrested and sent to a concentration camp shortly after Hitler was appointed chancellor in January of 1933. Although his father was eventually released, the family suffered much hardship throughout the twelve years of Nazi rule, which he wrote about directly in the prose piece "The Father" (1958).

After the war, Müller's father became a functionary of the Socialist Unity Party (SED), which had been created by merging the Communist and Social-Democratic parties after the war in the Russian occupied east of Germany. The SED became the ruling party when, in 1949, the (East) German Democratic Republic (GDR) was established. Having been elected mayor of a small town in Saxony, Müller's father soon got into trouble with his party and was expelled from it as a so-called "Titoist." This was a label invented by the Soviets to designate a follower of Josip Bronz Tito, the leader of the Yugoslavian Communist Party, which without the direct aid of either the Soviet Union or its western allies, drove the Nazis out of the Balkans. Much could be said about "Titoism," however, all we need to know for our purposes, is that Tito held that communism needed to be built based on conditions in each particular country rather than by strictly following the model established by the Soviet Union.

When his parents defected to the (West) German Federal Republic, in early 1951, the young Müller decided to stay in the GDR. He was fully committed to the young state's socialist agenda, which presented itself as a complete break with the fascist ideology of the past and offered the promise of a society free of the privileges and injustices of Germany's traditional class system. This decision set the course of Müller's life and established the context for the development of his plays and his cultural politics.

Müller moved to the GDR's capital, Berlin, where he tried hard to establish himself as a journalist, a poet and, eventually, playwright. The writings from those years reveal his firm belief in the future of socialism and the GDR, the only country that represented its German manifestation. He craved recognition by the cultural and intellectual elite of the young

East German state at a time, the 1950s, when its authorities labored to strictly circumscribe its ideological parameters. These were precarious years for any independent thinking or artistic experimentation since the government and the ruling party saw themselves imperiled as much from within as from their West German rival state. As the strikes and popular uprising in June 1953 clearly demonstrated, these fears were not misplaced. Müller applied several times between 1951 and 1954 to be accepted as a "master pupil of the Academy of the Arts" with Brecht, but was rejected each time.

During most of the 1950s, he struggled to make a living as a journalist and literary critic. Writing on issues of the day, he more or less adhered to what he understood to be the cultural/political views proscribed by the SED. Occasionally he blundered in his assessment of a repeatedly changing party line or unwittingly offended rival cultural factions, lapses that were not ignored, or forgotten, by the political and cultural authorities.

He had some early success with his first three plays—*Ten Days that Shook the World,* co-authored with Hagen Stahl (Müller, 2000. 65-108), *The Scab* (Müller/Weber 1989a: 23-56), and *The Correction* (Müller/Weber 2001: 30-42) all of which premiered in 1957 and 1958. The latter two conformed to the model of "Production Play," works that described problems as well as achievements of the young socialist industry, a cultural project strongly promoted through the party's cultural line. Stylistically they were reminiscent of Brecht. The two plays earned him and his then wife and collaborator, Inge Schwenkner, the coveted literary Heinrich Mann Prize. But soon he encountered serious setbacks.

In the autumn of 1961, shortly after the Berlin Wall had been established, Müller was facing accusations of being "a counterrevolutionary" who was trying to subvert the GDR's socialist system with his new play, *The Resettled Woman* (Müller 2000: 181-287). The text portrayed life in the East German countryside and the problems villagers had to cope with after the "land reform" of late 1945, when the large estates of the former Prussian aristocracy and other big landowners were carved up and distributed to farm workers, small farmers, and persons from the former German provinces east of the post-war Polish border. The play's title referred to the many ethnic Germans, who had been expelled from the newly annexed Polish territories and then resettled in small towns and villages of the two post-war German states. Müller believed that he had created a realistic yet positive representation of contemporary GDR village life and its various social conflicts. The authorities of party and state couldn't agree less, and the production was cancelled after one preview.

The consequence was Müller's expulsion from the Writers Association and a ban of all publications and stage performances of his work. (It wasn't until 1988, a year before the GDR's final implosion, that he was re-invited into the Association.) Though he delivered a somewhat groveling self-critique before his fellow writers at a special session of the Association, they none-the-less voted for his exclusion. Müller later explained that he had learned from Eisenstein, the early Soviet filmmaker, "who always volunteered to submit self-critiques. It enabled him to survive as an artist. [...] Being able to write was more important to me than my morals" (Müller 2005, Vol. 2: 140). Yet, for several years he was barely making a living by writing for East German radio and TV, mostly under an assumed pen-name.

His early texts indicate that Müller embraced the notion that any cultural production ought to advance the progress of the new socialist society, and that he felt this would require an honest depiction of the intricate dialectics that were complicating the development of socialist agriculture and industry. The authorities apparently felt threatened by such honesty. He later commented, "It was a continuous experience that everything I meant seriously, or considered to be good, was rejected" (Müller 2005, Vol. 2: 86). When the party eventually proclaimed that the GDR represented "the advanced form of existing Socialism," in 1967, the sixth year after the East German state had closed its borders, Müller saw this as, "the canonization of wretchedness, the birth of a travesty" (Müller 2005, Vol. 2: 157). Yet he preferred to continue living and working in the GDR, the socialist state that still held for him the promise of a better future, notwithstanding its dismal contemporary condition.

Until the mid-1960s his plays portrayed events, partly historical, partly fictional, from the past and present of socialism. They were written in a prose that has to be called "realistic" though the language often was poetic and rich in what Brecht called "gestus." Beginning with *The Resettled Woman*, he increasingly began to use free verse forms though still retaining segments of prose dialogue. He further explored this style in *The Construction Site* (Müller 2000: 329-396), another play about the difficulties that accompanied the building of a socialist industry in the GDR. It was the first major work he had been able to publish, three years after the *The Resettled Woman* affair. However, the text soon was denounced for its "lack of historical perspective" by Erich Honecker (who was to become the head of party and state six years later) during the 11th Plenum of the Party's Central Committee, in 1965, and the play's rehearsals had to be cancelled (Müller 2005, Vol.2: 156-57).

Thus discouraged from writing directly about contemporary issues, for a number of years Müller applied himself to revising narratives appropriated from classic Greek theater and mythology. Through these plays—*Philoctetes;* (Müller 2000: 289-327), *Oedipus Tyrant* (Müller 2004, Vol.1: 7-54), *Herakles 5* (Müller/Weber 1989a: 85-98), and *Prometheus* (Müller, 2001: 7-45)—Müller perfected his mastery of versified language and began to experiment with possibilities of a non-realistic treatment of fable and character. Except for two minor works, he never went back to the dramaturgy of his early plays that had emulated the model of Brecht's Epic Theater.

When, in the early 1970s, Müller returned to topics from the past and present of socialism, he took a far more critical view than during the 1950s and juxtaposed 20th Century events with earlier European and German history and mythology. His plays now clearly indicated a distanced position vis-à-vis the "advanced Socialism" that Honecker's GDR claimed to embody. The 1971 play *Germania Death in Berlin* (Müller/Weber, 1989b: 39-87) includes many scenes he had originally scripted during the 1950s, and it unfolds an ironic survey of German history from the end of World War I to the June of 1953 strikes in the GDR and the resultant popular uprising. The text comments on 20th Century history with scenes from the Niebelung myth and Frederick the Second's 18th Century Prussia. It could not be performed in East Germany until 1989, because its portrayal of the June 1953 events contradicted the official party narrative.

Nonetheless, Müller defended in interviews and on numerous other occasions his commitment to the GDR and published aggressive anti-Western statements. His continued adherence to the long-term goals of the communist experiment in the East, at this point, seems certain. At the same time, such proclamations of loyalty may also have helped to protect the travel privileges he had begun to enjoy after he had become an internationally acclaimed author during the 1970s. Starting with *Philoctetes,* at the Munich State Theatre in 1968, his plays were increasingly staged in the West, and not only in the Federal Republic but also in Switzerland and France. A first edition of his collected works was published in West Berlin in 1974, at a time when only few of his writings had been accepted for publication in the GDR. This, at the time, rather surprising success in the West was mainly due to the undeniable poetic quality of his texts and their often startling and perceptive views of past and present history, which seemed to resonate with western leftists.

Müller rejected the Lessing-Prize stipend he had been awarded by the Senate of the West German city state of Hamburg in 1971, arguing that he didn't want to share the prize with the fellow recipient, Max Horkheimer of the Frankfurt School, who, he said, is "separated from me not merely by a border between [the two German] states." This was, as he later admitted, a public maneuver at a time when he badly needed permission to travel to Bulgaria to marry his third wife, Ginka Cholakova (Müller 2005, Vol. 2: 280-281). At the same time, such public political statements, were often responses to West German propaganda directed against the GDR in the prevailing Cold War climate.

It is no surprise that Müller's loyalty to the GDR was frequently labeled as rank opportunism by Western critics, since most of his royalties were derived from publications and performances in the West while he was holding positions as a playwright-in-residence with theaters in East Berlin, such as the Berliner Ensemble (1970-76) and the Volksbühne (1976-82). He responded that he was "living in the material he was writing about," namely the city divided by the Berlin Wall. He liked to characterize the Wall as the cemented metaphor for a world that the Cold War had frozen into mutually hostile camps:

> The GDR is important for me since all the lines of separation in our world traverse that country. That is the real situation of [today's] world, and it is quite concretely evidenced by the Berlin Wall. In the GDR there exists a much harsher pressure of experience than here [West Germany, at the time of the quoted interview] and...the pressure of experience is the prerequisite for [my] writing.
> (Müller 1986: 135).

In the 1970s and 80s, his stage texts moved further and further away from addressing the specific culture and politics he had to live with in the "advanced socialist" society of the GDR. Increasingly, they focus on the complicated dialectics that are driving the motion of history, embodied for Müller by the image of the "hapless angel" as he described him in a prose-poem of 1958. The angel is being buried under the debris of the past tumbling down in his back, while the wind from the future is choking him with his own breath and exploding his eyeballs. He is buried "waiting for history in the petrifcation of flight vision breath. Until the renewed whirring of powerful wings will move in waves through the stone and signify his flight" (Müller/Weber 2001: 79). The image was borrowed (if greatly rephrased) from Walter Benjamin's comment on a drawing by Paul Klee. It articulated Müller's belief that humanity's progress was increasingly stifled in his own time and that there might be a long hiatus before it would become possible to revive history's revolutionary mission.

It has been argued that Müller's first visit to the United States was critical in changing his perception of the ideological discourse of the time.

In particular, his American sojourn (1975/76) reinforced views that had become conspicuous in his writings since the early 1960s. The militant feminism he encountered in the U.S. reinforced analogous views he had articulated in several of his plays including *The Construction Site* and *Cement* (1973). He was considering at the time an adaptation of Aristophanes' *Lysistrata* that, judging from the few completed fragments (Weber 2005: 117) anticipated the aggressive feminist vision which later informed the Ophelia segments of *Hamletmachine*, a stage text he conceived after his return from America. In a conversation we had the year after his first visit to the U.S., Müller emphasized that an American production of the text should center on Ophelia rather than Hamlet, since it would relate much more directly to the contemporaneous social context of the U.S. A number of feminist intellectuals considered his writings as misogynistic since they resented the violence, and often brutality, his plays assign to many of their female characters as, for instance, Ophelia and Medea. Yet, "He [Müller] always insisted on showing conflicts unsparingly and resisted to offer harmonious solutions," as Janine Ludwig, the German Müller scholar, has argued (Lehmann/Primavesi 2005: 75). In a culture that embraces compromise and "feel-good" politics, as U.S. society usually tends to do, Müller's uncompromising positions couldn't but provoke disapproval.

The monumental landscapes he encountered while traveling in the U.S. provided "the fundamental experience" of his sojourn, as he later stated in his autobiography: "Everywhere there is landscape that isn't yet occupied [...] landscapes which won't be domesticated" (Müller 2005, Vol. 2: 223). The experience made him realize that geography had a pervasive impact on human history, an impact at least as important as the shifts in the political and economic environment that he previously had privileged in his writings, living, as he did, within the narrow confines of a small country in Central Europe. His new insights became immediately tangible in the text he worked on during his visit and completed after his return from America.

Gundling's Life Frederick of Prussia Lessing's Sleep Dream Scream (Müller/Weber 1984: 59-78) examined the position of intellectuals and their concomitant abuse in Prussian history. Müller's "Prussia" might well have been perceived at the time as a stand-in for the GDR. The play also commented on the Enlightenment's ascendance and eventual failure, as exemplified by the socio-political systems (both capitalist and socialist) that proclaimed their dedication to Enlightenment/modernist precepts. Müller began here to use specific landscapes as metaphoric images in his critique of the Enlightenment and its misuse when it was invoked to justify the atrocities inflicted in its name during the last centuries of human "pre-history."

While his subsequent work, *Hamletmachine* (Müller/Weber 1984: 49-58), was mainly concerned with the history of post World War II Europe, and especially of Central Europe, it clearly reflected, as I have indicated, the American experience as well. The text marked a turning point in Müller's oeuvre. At first, critics were hesitant to even perceive it as a play, but it was soon recognized as a new beginning, portent of Müller's emancipation from his previous dramaturgic model—Brecht's—as much as from the ideological positions he hitherto had shared with Brecht. *Hamletmachine* presented a direly detached perspective of the Cold War world of the time, a position that was equally critical of the socialist and the capitalist versions of contemporary society. As a performance text it represented a complete break with familiar modes of Western theater, venturing much further than the previous texts that he had labeled "synthetic fragments" to mark their deliberate disregard of linear narrative and formal consistency. *Hamletmachine*'s bitter assessment of the quandaries that afflicted both sides of a Europe divided by the Berlin Wall, begins with the sentence uttered by the protagonist claiming, "I was Hamlet" (meaning actually Heiner Müller, as several critics immediately proposed?) who is talking to the sea while he has turned his back on the "ruins of Europe." This opening sentence seemed to hint at Müller's resolve to move his focus away from European topics. And though the text is for the most part concerned with the history of a Europe that has been torn apart by the Cold War, it frequently returns to topics of American consumer society.

Müller's ensuing play, *The Task* (Müller/Weber 1984: 81-101), is his first (and only) text situated explicitly outside of Europe, in colonial Jamaica. Its complex non-linear narrative involves three emissaries of revolutionary France who find themselves stranded after Napoleon's rise to power and his repudiation of the idea of a world-wide revolution, a quite obvious parallel to Stalin's dismissal of Trotsky's concept of world revolution during the 1920s. The protagonist is the intellectual Debuisson, a former colonialist slaveholder who joined the French Revolution in protest against slavery and the privileges his family derived from it. In the end, he returns to the family, disgusted with the excesses and eventual failure of the revolution and dismissing the idea of sacrifice in the name of the revolution's humanistic project.

As in *Gundling's Life...* and *Hamletmachine*, Müller interrogates and judges, quite harshly, the intentions and choices of intellectuals who enter into a complex and often self-delusional interaction with politics and state power, a theme that appears in many of his texts written during the '70s, '80s and '90s. It probably is no accident that the topic of the intellectuals' relationship to their contemporaneous political rulers appeared in Müller's writings at a time when he had to cope with the increasing attention of the "Stasi" (short for Ministerium für Staatsicherheit/Ministry for State Security, East Germany's equivalent of the FBI and the CIA combined). He was invited to collaborate with the security apparatus and, knowing refusal would deprive him of the right to travel and lead to his constant observation by the Stasi, Müller agreed to do so. Yet, as the now accessible files of the former Stasi have revealed, he never denunciated any person but rather tried to use these contacts to influence the cultural politics of the GDR and also to protect friends and young writers who had become suspect to the authorities (Müller 2005, Vol. 2: 390-407).

Starting in 1980, Müller began increasingly to direct and, like Brecht in his final years after his return to Germany from exile, channeled much of his creative energy into the staging of his plays, mainly at the Volksbühne and Deutsches Theater in East Berlin. By this time, it had become possible to present the criticism of the GDR implied in his texts with little intervention from the cultural authorities. They had become more tolerant in many respects, partly due, it seems, to the ascendance of Gorbatchev in the Soviet Union but also, as Müller has argued, to their awareness that the GDR was heading towards its demise. Thus he could stage a production of *Hamlet,* in his own translation, combined with *Hamletmachine,* which had finally been published in the GDR in 1988. He created an eight-hour performance at Deutsches Theater. Rehearsals started in November of 1989 when the ruling SED was still in control of the government. The production premiered after the destruction of the Wall and the party's resultant loss of power, in March 1990. In October the GDR was absorbed by the (West) German Federal Republic. The production demonstrated, as he phrased it, that "the Old will be the New for a long time to come."

To Müller's mind/politic, the unification of Germany was not a desirable achievement. "From one servitude to another, from Stalin to Deutsche Bank," as he put it (Müller 1994: 87). He took a decidedly skeptical view of the concept and contemporaneous implementation of what those in the West called democracy: "There is no such thing as democracy. That is merely a fiction. It is, as always, an oligarchy, and democracy never has functioned in any other way. There are [always] a few who are living at the expense of the many... And that is today's situation. I cannot be ecstatic about freedom and democracy" (Müller, 2005, Vol. 2: 402-403).

The texts written in the few remaining years of his life express his profound disappointment with socialism's self-inflicted collapse and an innate disgust with capitalism's global conquest, as *Mommsen's Block* and *Ajax for Instance* make evident (Müller/Weber 2001: 122-129; 154-160).

Nonetheless, those final years were a period of unprecedented popular success for Müller. He received many prestigious German and European literary awards, and the 1990 Experimenta theater festival in Frankfurt was dedicated to his lifetime achievement, presenting more than twenty productions of his plays from several European countries. He was elected President of the East German Academy of the Arts and mediated successfully the contested merger with its Western counterpart. In 1993, he directed Wagner's *Tristan and Isolde* at the Bayreuth Festival, to remarkable acclaim. After having staged several of his own plays while being a member of a collective of directors at the Berliner Ensemble since 1992, he was appointed artistic director of the company in 1995, attaining the mantle of his erstwhile model Brecht. His last directorial achievement was the staging of Brecht's *The Resistible Rise of Arturo Ui*, a resounding success that was still in the repertory of the Berliner Ensemble, eleven years after Müller's death. He also became a public personality, much sought after for interviews and televised debates as, for instance, his 1993 discussion with West German writer and filmmaker Alexander Kluge, *The Death of Seneca,* so named because at the end Müller reads his poem of the same name (Müller/Weber 2001: 161-169).

Müller certainly didn't devote his life to achieving such a public career. As he stated during the last of his many published conversations, ten weeks before he died of cancer, "Art lives of insecurity, includes risks; otherwise it is of no interest." He also emphasized: "Theater won't be interesting at all unless you do what you cannot do. That is the only way something new can be created" (Müller/Weber, 2001: 229). He always had regarded theater as a laboratory where the collective imagination of a society is/becomes productive. And rejecting the frequent claims that the theatre is in a "crisis" he posited: "Theatre *is* crisis. It is the definition of crisis—or should be. It can only function as crisis and in a crisis, or it has no relation whatsoever to the society outside the theater walls" (Müller/Weber 2001: 232).

An intrinsic consequence of such notions was Müller's attitude regarding productions of his plays by other directors. Quite in contrast, for instance, to Beckett and Brecht, who both insisted that their works should be staged close to the way they themselves directed them or had prescribed their staging, Müller granted unfettered liberties to the directors of future productions. He firmly held that any text, when being staged, had to be read anew and performed in a manner that responds to the historical moment and would challenge the audience to consider and possibly reexamine their own societal/historical context.

Müller often affirmed that in his theater the spectators are invited to "work," i.e. are being pushed into the role of co-creators of the performance they are watching. The theater—addressing rather small groups, compared with other performance media—should create a free space where audiences are encouraged to exercise their imagination. That is, of course, a proposition originally associated with Brecht's concept of theater. However, Brecht did not anticipate the dominance the technological media would have achieved by the end of his century. Müller, having witnessed the encompassing triumph of film and television, concluded that theater ought to contest "the imperialist occupation and liquidation of the human imagination through the pre-fabricated clichés and standards of the media [...] That is a primary political task, even if the [media's] content is not at all concerned with political issues" (Müller 1982: 177).

Observing the mass media of the early 21st century, one would hardly disagree with his claim that, "Forgetting is counter-revolutionary since all technology is geared towards the extinction of memory" (Müller/Weber 2001: 135). The emergence of generations whose minds were washed clean of any awareness of history, of populations who are living only in the here and now, clearly troubled Müller: "More and more reality is eliminated by virtual reality [...] the arts have to resist that" (Müller 1994: 215). For Müller an awareness and engagement of history was essential for continued human development, and that, more than any specific political attitude or ideological stance, was his cultural politic.

This is but a brief summary of what Hans-Thies Lehmann has called Müller's "zig-zag movement between the ideological camps of his time," (Lehmann/Primavesi 2005: 12). In a period of ideological confusion and the apparent discrediting of the Enlightenment and the ideologies it engendered, Müller has been celebrated as a postmodernist playwright and thinker who rejects the precepts of the Enlightenment. Yet, I would argue that a close reading of his writings, in all their diversity, will reveal that he never completely rejected the modernist project that embraced the Enlightenment's intentions, notwithstanding all his criticism of the abuses and flawed efforts that claimed, or were accused of, having implemented the Enlightenment's vision.

When I began an interview with Müller, in the early 1980s, with the question of what he would consider as postmodern drama, Müller replied, referring to an Expressionist German dramatist who was killed in 1915 in

World War I: "The only postmodernist I know of was August Stramm, a modernist who worked in a post office" (Müller/Weber 1984: 137). His tongue-in-cheek remark indicates Müller's disdain of any label that is trying to confine him to trendy fashions, be they of ideology, literature, or critical theory.

In 1986, Müller penned a brief Haiku-like poem for Bonnie Marranca, the publisher of his writings in America:

Without hope
Without despair
For the next half century.
(Marranca 1988: 20)

It succinctly expresses his view during the decade that ended with what has been regarded as socialism's ultimate failure. Twenty years later, he probably would be less optimistic. I am wondering what future time span he might be citing today.

Work Cited

Lehmann, Hans-Thies and Primavesi, Patrick (2005). *Heiner Müller Handbuch*, Stuttgart-Weimar: Verlag J.B.Metzler.

Marranca, Bonnie (1988). "Despoiled Shores. Heiner Müller's *Natural History* Lessons." *Performing Arts Journal* 10, New York: PAJ Publications.

Müller, Heiner (1982). *Rotwelsch*. Berlin: Merve Verlag.

—. (1986). *Gesammelte Irrtümmer, Interviews und Gespräche.* Frankfurt am Main: Verlag der Autoren.

—. (1994). *Gesammelte Irrtümer 3. Texte und Gespräche.* Frankfurt am Main: Verlag der Autoren.

—. (1998, 1999, 2000, 2001, 2002, 2004, 2005, 2 Vol.). *Werke.* Frankfurt am Main: Suhrkamp Verlag,

Müller, Heiner and Weber, Carl (1984). *Hamletmachine and other Texts for the Stage.* New York: Performing Arts Journal Publications.

— .(1989a). *The Battle, Plays, Prose, Poems.* New York: Performaing Arts Journal Publications.

—. (1989b). *Explosion of a Memory.* New York: Performing Arts Journal Publications.

—. (2001). *A Heiner Müller Reader.* Baltimore and London: Johns Hopkins University Press.

Weber, Carl (2005). "Heiner Müller's Lysistrata Experiment." *Performing Arts Journal,* Vol. 27, No. 1.

CHAPTER TWO

THE DISSIDENT'S DILEMMA: MÜLLER'S CHOICE TO STAY IN EAST GERMANY

ALEKSANDAR SASHA LUKAC

While I have directed works by Heiner Müller both in my native Yugoslavia where I served as artistic director at the National Theatre in Belgrade, Theatre Zoran Radmilovic and the independent political theatre, Plexus Boris Piljnjak, as well as in my adopted home of Canada, and have been teaching and researching theatre and related subjects for fifteen years at York University in Toronto and McMaster University in Hamilton, my connection to the great German playwright is more political and personal than scholarly or aesthetic. We both came to maturity as theatre artists in the old "communist" bloc of Eastern Europe. We each remained, at least in our own estimations, politically progressive. We each faced the question of whether to stay within our nominally socialist homelands or to defect to the West. We both stayed until those countries, as we knew them, ceased to exist—the German Democratic Republic (GDR) absorbed into a greater Germany, and the Socialist Federal Republic of Yugoslavia fractured into many pieces. I did eventually decide to leave my country during the worst times of political upheaval in the early nineties to settle in the refreshingly subtle political and cultural contexts of Canada. Thus, this essay is colored by the very real experience of a political artist in exile. It is from the vantage point of some 15 years of exile that I will attempt to look at the complex and sometimes contradictory evidence used to contextualize Müller's refusal to leave East Germany.

Müller's choice not to leave his homeland gains in ethical, philosophical and political weight in view of the many examples of well-known artists who donned the dissident identity and left for the West during the Cold War. The short history of East Germany provides an abundance of examples illustrating the trend towards exile, not only among artists and other public figures, but within the population in general. The fact that these attempts were often brutally suppressed and their perpetrators severely punished raises a variety of questions over the choice of someone, such as Müller, who had every opportunity to leave. It is well known that Müller stubbornly refused to follow this path despite the many opportunities to do so. However, the apparent mystery that shrouds such a decision, as well as the various suspicions it continues to provoke, arguably sheds more light on the bias of the critics' perspectives than on Müller's possible reasons.

Instead of speculating on Müller's possible personal, psychological or political reasons for remaining in the GDR (speculations I am not qualified to make even should I consider them helpful), I propose to analyze this "mystery" from two observation points: 1) the specific nature of the artist's position under the communist regimes of Eastern Europe; and 2) an analysis of the perspectives of cultural re-positioning of a political artist in new political and cultural environments. This approach intends to locate Müller's decision firmly in the context of the relation of an artist and his art to the society in which/for which it was created.

Müller in the Cold War/the Cold War in Müller

The defining moment in the history of Eastern Europe, including Yugoslavia and East Germany, is the Second World War and its political aftermath. The popular notion is that the world was split into two sides, the West and the East, each represented by and representative of a clear set of economic, political and ethical philosophies. It is not necessary here to dwell on the narrowness of the idea of the whole world represented and contained by the discourse of only two of its continents—Europe and North America. That said, the Cold War did provide an illusion of clarity, not only of the divisions between the two, but, even more so, the lines of allegiance within the two sides. From today's perspectives the old demarcations seem to be too convenient and, what is more, often quite imprecise and simply untrue. The need for clarity is understandable from the perspective of fighting a war, particularly given the fact that the conflicts of World War II had quickly metamorphosed into the Cold War discourse of communism versus capitalism, which, of course, had preceded the war and had not been resolved by it. This clarity of division/allegiance was emphasized and perpetuated by the propaganda machines on both sides, often with extremely damaging and confusing effects on the issues of both collective and individual identities of the respective populations contained within these artificially constructed

domains. This is the context in which Müller wrote. His work, I will
suggest, might be understood as an attempt to move beyond the "clarity"
of the Cold War. His ability to engage the political, ideological and artistic
oversimplifications not only of East German culture but of Cold War
culture in general is, I hope to show, tied to his decision to remain behind
the Wall.

The ideologically imposed simplicities of the Cold War might have
been less evident in the Western countries whose political cultures were
older, more supple and sophisticated than those of the barely-born
"communist" states. That said, the public in the West, to a large extent,
accepted the Manichaean dichotomy of the Cold War and viewed the
regimes of Eastern Europe as evil and virtually all the same. In my
frequent travels to the West during the Cold War, I had all too many
opportunities to explain the finer differences between Czechoslovakia and
Yugoslovakia (sic) despite the popular belief created by apparatchiks in
Yugoslavia that our anti-Soviet stands were well noted and even
celebrated abroad.

The fact of the matter was that in the Eastern Bloc the imposed
ideological unity of the various Communist Parties and nation-states
masked the struggles of various countries and national minorities for what
they felt were their specific national identities against both the Soviet
Union's conscious attempts to blur them and to substitute a single identity
based on a political ideology, and the West's ironically complicit
willingness to do the same albeit for completely different reasons. The end
of the imposed simplicities of "communism" brought to the surface the
repressed nationalistic tensions of the previous sixty years—as the
collapse of Yugoslavia and the continuing war in Chechnya illustrate in
the extreme.

(The ideological and political simplicities of the Cold War also
covered over ongoing conflicts in the West. The current social tensions
brought about by the influx of immigrants from the impoverished South
testify to the fact that, despite its victory relative to the dichotomies of the
Cold War, all is not quiet on the Western Front. The long-standing
division along the lines of, ultimately economic, concepts of capitalism
and communism, seems to have postponed, by the virtue of its simplicity
and feigned universality, the discourse on a multitude of issues, among
them racism, entitlement to a good life according to geographical
allocation and cultural identity.)

To understand Müller's decision to stay on the eastern side of the Wall,
we need to unpack some of the differences between the various "people's

democracies" of the East and Müller's particular relation to the history and politics of the GDR.

Thus, while World War II was the defining event of 20th Century European history, it did not impact in exactly the same ways on every country in the Eastern Bloc. Each country had a specific relationship to fascism and its defeat. The contrast between Yugoslavia and East Germany, for example is striking in this regard. The GDR was lead by German communists who survived the war as exiles in the Soviet Union. In essence, it was a state imposed by the conquering Russian Army. (Müller looked at some of the consequences of trying to build a socialism that is imposed from the top down with a population that had been organized by Nazism in his early plays, in particular *The Scab* and *The Correction.*) By contrast, in Yugoslavia socialism was established through the Communist Party's leadership of the guerrilla war against the German occupation. That is, it grew out of a grassroots-based insurgency that succeeded in liberating the country and was not dependent on the military might of the Soviet Union.

One result of this was that Yugoslavs (including its artists) tended to understand fascism as a foreign movement imposed by Nazi invaders that the Yugoslav people of all ethnicities had heroically defeated with their blood and courage. In retrospect, this perspective conveniently ignored the various native fascist movements and ways of thinking that never fully disappeared and re-emerged with such viciousness after 1989. However, that was the national myth that shaped our understanding of ourselves and our government. We viewed the communist regime as a part of a historic natural progression toward a better, more humane world. (This Marxist narrative was overlaid on the much older Christian narrative of sacrifice and redemption.) To the East Germans, arguably, the communist regime was a military occupation that immediately followed Nazism. Many East Germans viewed themselves as part of a nation divided and sandwiched between two dictatorships, forced to reconcile contradictory views of national and political identity brought about by such a close and forceful proximity of titanic governmental and ideological systems. These different histories/political realities led to different approaches to examining history and society in the theatre. While Yugoslavia turned, for the most part, to its own version of Theatre of the Absurd and satire, Müller and his colleagues in the GDR produced something grimmer.

At least since Romanticism, art in the Western cultural continuum has been considered an intuitive means of understanding humanity and helping to humanize us. Müller, looking at German history with unblinking eyes, implicitly challenged this romantic/humanistic assumption:

> A nation has to have access to its historical background. A collective
> memory of the nation cannot be denied. A nation's very existence is in
> jeopardy if its memory and history are erased. ... To free oneself from the
> historical nightmare one has to first acknowledge that history exists. One
> has to learn it; otherwise it may resurrect itself in the old fashioned manner
> of Hamlet's ghost. History needs to be first analyzed before it can be
> denunciated and overcome. (Müller 1982: 58)

Thus, given the nightmare of German (and world) history, Müller
faced the formidable task of wrestling with all of the political and
historical currents that seemed to successfully deny the assumption of the
humanity of art (or of the human species). In fact, from his observation
point, the forces of destruction and alienation of all things human must
have appeared so overwhelming that he had to consider the possibility that
they are not antagonistic to human nature but an essential part of it. Maybe
even its very essence.

Although the Second World War brought the potential bestiality of the
human species to the forefront, Muller's examination of German history
was not limited exclusively to the events and issues raised by the war.
Vlado Obad in his essay "Constructive Defeatism" argues that Müller's
uniqueness amongst the other East German (and not only them) writers is
his attempt to investigate the German national myths stemming from the
Prussian, through the fascist and finally to the Stalinist renditions,
observing them in the context of a continuum, not as separate "phases"
independent of each other. Thus, fascism and eventually Stalinism were
observed as a natural progression from Prussia's simultaneous de-
intellectualization and militarization of Germany. (Obad 1985a: 42)

It is obvious how this view of German history would be considered
quite problematic in East German political culture where socialist realism
was the predominant aesthetic and where art was expected to project a
definite optimism about the world and its progress. (Of course, this
progress was only manifest in select parts of the world, such as the GDR
and the Soviet Union, where the "right kind" of socialist revolution had
won.) Müller's attempt to dissect history and methodically observe all of
the painful details of the past, as possible evidence of the disease that the
whole world is suffering from, was not considered a pragmatic or positive
approach, despite its roots in Marxist methodology. The Stalinist
government was not interested in the discoveries revealed by such an
investigation, unless they could be incorporated in the larger body of its
ideological assumptions. A connection between the past and present
without the acknowledgment of the qualitative changes brought about by
the communist revolution was essentially oppositional (or at least not in

sync with) official doctrine. This created many problems for Müller whose works were in perpetual danger of being (and sometimes were) banned. He spent much of the decade of the sixties unable to get his work produced or published in the GDR.

Perhaps what saved him from even harder consequences was the fact that he was equally suspicious of Germany's imperial and capitalist past, as well as West Germany's capitalist present. This essentially rendered his process void of an ideological juxtaposition—Müller, at least in his texts for the stage—did not seem to be interested in proving either side "right" or "better." And as much as his approach resembled the Marxist analysis of history, he felt free to veer away from it and establish his own methodologies drawing on other philosophers as well as other playwrights—most importantly through the deconstruction of the Greeks and Shakespeare. In that context, Obad also understands Müller's most significant break with Brecht to be his rejection of the orthodox Marxist concept of history as a progressive process directly reliant on the continuous advancement of production methodologies. (Obad 1985a: 45)

Müller's anti-ideological approach essentially removed him from the most common dissident discourse. Both the East and the West understood quite early that they were dealing with a mind interested in an approach to history that would be equally dangerous, or at least uncomfortable, to either side precisely because it was not overdetermined by an ideological filter and purported that history is the real activity of real people, not a figment of one's political or social imagination. For Müller, our present state of being is only a point in the historic continuum, not a final destination (or a step toward a predetermined final destination) produced by the ideological superiority of one concept over the others. Essentially, Müller's approach rendered his "case" larger than the ultimately petty daily politics of "dissidentship." As much as his movement in either direction would have been temporarily greeted with enthusiasm and a probable claim of a small political victory, his actual presence would cause more problems than that victory's worth. His plays, especially the later ones, hardly contained any easily exploitable thematic or ideological content. They were not plays with classical structures, accessible imagery, and least of all, clear "messages" that could be conveniently repackaged for propaganda purposes.

Müller's refusal to play the role of dissident protected him from full scale persecution in the East and distanced him from the embrace of Cold Warriors in the West, thus playing an important role in keeping him living—and working—in the GDR.

Exile and/or Engagement?

Exile is difficult for anyone. That said, some types of artists—dancers, painters, composers and musicians—have a reasonable chance of earning a living with their craft and even gaining public recognition in a foreign country. However, for artists for whom language and the examination of social conflict is essential—that is, for playwrights and the actors and directors who work with the playwright's language and structured conflicts—exile can be economically and creatively deadly.

Recently, at a conference on Art in Exile held at the University of Toronto, Goran Stefanovski, the renowned Macedonian playwright, currently living between England and his native Macedonia, recounted his conversations about business strategies with his English literary agent. At the end of a long conversation he was warned that the window of opportunity to cash in on his notoriety within Yugoslav circles was rapidly diminishing with the acceleration of the peace process in the Balkans. He shared his disappointment with the agent's cynical approach with another expatriate—the great Serbo-Croatian actor Rade Sherbegia who has in recent years made a career out of playing various generic Eastern Europeans in movies that range from *The Saint, Eyes Wide Shut* to *Snatch*, and least but not last, the teenage comedy *Euro Trip*. Stefanovski lamented:

> …Now I live in Canterbury, in a small rustic world, in a tourist place with a cathedral. The main street has a comic book store that sells American novelties. The window boasts a full-size cutout of a hero of the popular Sci-Fi series Babylon 5. It is a photo of a creature with a glowing halo around its forehead. I know the woman who is playing this character. Her name is Mira Furlan. At one time she was one of the best actresses of Yugoslav film and television. She was both the protagonist and the heroine of "our story." Now she is an extraterrestrial. She has become the stereotype of Eastern European. (Stefanovski: 1)

While many an actor would consider this fantastic success—for both Furlan and especially Sherbegia this is quite a spiral downward. His current roles, even if lucrative, are below the heights of being recognized as the best Yugoslav *Hamlet* and even more importantly, as one of the leaders of the internationally renowned KPGT. KPGT was the theatre that had created a mini revolution in the late seventies and early eighties with its willingness to produce the most controversial political plays of the time while hiring the best Yugoslav actors. When Stefanovski pointed out that Sherbegia had turned from playing protagonists to playing the antagonists for the Western cinema and that this recent career illustrates what has happened to "our story," Sherbegia replied that maybe we didn't really have a story worth telling. (Stefanovski: 2)

In order to understand the full connotations of this anecdote one has to understand that both the public and their peers held these men in the highest esteem. They were the cultural elite—as Müller, despite the twists and turns in his relationship with the government, had been in the GDR. They were the political and theatrical avant-garde, the role models for many a young artist.

Heiner Müller had the opportunity to consider the option of exile many times in his travels to the West. Yet he never availed himself of the opportunity. Why? As he put it in an interview with Sylvère Lotringer in 1981:

> People brought up here [GDR] have at least an image, or a hope, for another society, for another kind of living. This image is linked to the end of the commodity world. In the West, this world is in full bloom, and you can never really get accustomed to that. Many of my friends moved to the West—writers especially. They tried to write there, but it's really a problem. You can never forget the image of another world. That becomes their schizophrenia. (Müller 1990: 14)

In a sense, Müller's genius can be explained by his recognition and engagement of the specific dynamics created by the inherent artificiality of a state suspended in an invented and ultimately (as history would prove) impossible context. Yet that impossible context was the inspiration and the material of his work. On some level, at least, he seems to have been aware that leaving the GDR would have been tantamount to divorcing his muse.

That muse was fundamentally political. Müller's art is the product of a poet committed to a communist utopia faced with a terribly deformed and clearly failing socialist experiment. The GDR was one of the most Stalinist of the Soviet Bloc nations, which, perhaps ironically, gave art there a particular power. In contrast to my native Yugoslavia where there was a more decentralized economy in which factories had some latitude in self-management and profit sharing, in the GDR everything, including cultural production, was centralized. In the Yugoslavian theatre "decentralization" took the particularly perfidious form of the regime insisting that all decisions concerning the banning of theatrical productions did not come from above, but were left in the hands of the Communist Party members within the theatre companies. While this generated the appearance of a more open society, it, in fact, led to an insidious auto-censorship. Müller faced no such decentralization. Culture, like everything else in the GDR, was administered from the top down. Thus, to the extent that his plays engaged and challenged the simplicities of the Cold War, they were an engagement and challenge of the political culture (and the political leadership) of the entire nation. When his play *The Resettled Woman* was banned in 1961, it led not to Müller self-censoring his next play, but to his expulsion from the Writers Association and the banning of the staging or publishing of any of his texts. In this context, every play was a political act. When speaking of the impact of art in the two Germanys, Müller said, "Everything you write in the East is very important. You have a hard time being published here because it has such impact." (Müller 1990: 15)

As an artist both supportive of the attempt to build socialism and, at the same time, critical of what he considered the stunted "actually existing socialism" in the GDR, his work was an ongoing interface with the society he was simultaneously supportive of and repulsed by. He understood that his provocations would engender push back. As he put it in an interview with Horst Laube in 1980, "If the role of drama is to bring society to its limits, then it simultaneously provokes all restorative powers who absolutely want to retain these limits. It doesn't even have to be the police or the state. Most people's lives are based on maintaining those limits, whether in private or public." (Müller 1990: 196).

Müller could probably have made more money in the West, and, at least initially, he likely would have generated a great many productions and a good deal of acclaim. Yet in the context of the commodified society of the West his works would have lost their power of social/political engagement that the conditions of the GDR provided. It is clear that Müller was aware that his artistic inspiration and political mission were inseparable from the political culture and history of the GDR. Fleeing to the West would have not only have lessened the impact but altered the very nature of his work.

The artist stays, the country disappears

In the end, of course, Müller never left the GDR, the GDR left him— and the stage of history. His exile, like mine, came from the disappearance of our countries.

Obviously the fall of the Berlin Wall forced Müller to face qualitatively new political circumstances. How well, as an artist and a politically-engaged individual, he dealt with these circumstance can be debated. That he was not happy about them is clear from, among other things, one of his last texts, *Mommsen's Block*, where he describes sitting in a four-star restaurant in Berlin listening to two men at a neighboring table:

Two heroes of the new times dined at the next table
Zombies of capital brokers and traders
And as I listened to their dialogue greedy
To feed my disgust with the Here and Now
//
Five streets away as the police sirens indicate
The poor are clobbering the poorest
And when the gentlemen turned to private matters Cigars and Cognac
Strictly according to the textbooks of Political Economics
Of Capitalism:
//
Animal sounds Who would write that down
With passion Hate is a waste Contempt an empty exercise...
(Müller 2001: 128-129)

It is significant, I think, that Muller decided to continue rehearsals of *Hamlet/Machine*, his staging of Shakespeare's *Hamlet* with his own *Hamletmachine* at the Deutsches Theater, even while the Wall was falling. In doing so, he demonstrated an attitude that informed all of his work— that his art *was* his political statement/activity. He made it clear that his art was never secondary; it came before any political event, however exhilarating or catastrophic. He thus avoided the vast vacuum encountered by those who embrace political change as final. The fall of the GDR was just one point on the ongoing historical continuum. An exile in his own city, he continued to say what he thought he needed to say—even if the political environment in which he was saying it had changed overnight.

The work of exiled artists so often falls into a severe turbulence of political and economic circumstances far exceeding their own powers of perception, let alone control. Unless it is firmly rooted in at least one "known" element of the equation, it has a great chance of being completely disengaged from both its original source and its intended audience. The paradox of Müller's success is that his "known" element was the most improbable state of East Germany—a country that constantly defied logical analysis and was submerged in permanent anticipation of demise. I would argue that his tactic of resisting the urge to leave East Germany proved to be vital to the development and evaluation of his work.

To those of us—theatre artists and others—who lived our lives in the midst of the rise and fall of 20th century communism, Müller will continue to occupy a special place.

How theatrical and literary history deal with Müller's "impossible" texts born of the "impossible" situation that was the GDR, of course, remains to be seen. All that can be said with any certainty is that the impossible political situation and the impossible art are inextricably connected. To those who ask why he never left the GDR, all that can be said is: be grateful that he didn't.

Work Cited

Muller, Heiner (1982). *Rotwelsch*. Berlin: Merve Verlag.
—. (1990). *Germania*. Ed. Sylveré Lotringer. Trans. Bernard and Caroline Schütze. New York: Semiotext(e).
—. (2001). A Heiner Müller Reader. Ed. and trans. Carl Weber. Baltimore and London: The John Hopkins University Press.
Obad, Vlado (1985a). "Constructive Defeatism." 1. Zagreb: *Prolog/teorija/tekstovi*: 42-50.
—.(1985b). "Muller's Work At The National Theatre." Zagreb: *Prolog/teorija/tekstovi*: 61-62.
Stefanovski, Goran. "Theatre and Exile Conference." *Toronto Slavic Quarterly*. March 21-22, 2002.

CHAPTER THREE

A CANCER WALK THROUGH GERMAN HISTORY

EVA BRENNER

The Universal German

Heiner Müller is very much a German writer, not only because the dramatic and poetic styles and traditions he draws on—from Buchner through Brecht—are overwhelmingly German, but because his ultimate theme—which haunts even texts set elsewhere—is the horror of German history. Taken as a whole, Müller's work is a contemplation of the reoccurring failures of German history, reaching back to the Peasant Wars of the 16th century, the failure of the democratic revolution of 1848, the aborted Spartacist (communist) Uprising of 1919, and the ignoble collapse in 1989 of the imposed-revolution-from-above known as the German Democratic Republic. In Müller's work German history appears as an uninterrupted chain of senseless and deadly war-games, an accumulation of slaughter, fratricide and repression.

As Müller put it in an interview with Sylvère Lotringer in 1988, "I was born into a civil war, I live in a civil war and there is still a civil war" (Müller 1990: 83). That civil war, often open and violent, sometimes repressed and simmering, has resulted in a kind of cultural schizophrenia in German culture. (Here and throughout this paper, I use "German" not just to refer to Germany per se, but all of German speaking central Europe in as far as it is influenced by Germany.) German cultural schizophrenia— the Marxist legacy/the fascist legacy, revolution/counter-revolution, cosmopolitanism/nationalism, high culture/base atrocity, the East/the West—is evident not only in the plays, such as the *Germania* series, that are explicitly about German history, but in virtually all of Müller's texts, including those considered his masterpieces, such as *Hamletmachine* (1978) and *The Task* (1979).

As a political playwright and a German, Müller took it as his job to take us on, "a cancer walk through German history" (Schödel 1993:57). In his short essay, "I Want To Be A German" (1985), Müller wrote of the Germans as, "A people castrated of its civil courage by the bloody repression of a premature revolution [the Peasant Wars, a proto-communist uprising of German peasants led by Thomas Müntzer, 1524-1525] and a resulting thirty-year war, whose spine was crushed by the beheading of its proletariat through the murder of two of its Jewish leaders forgotten by the majority [Karl Liebknecht and Rosa Luxemburg, the assassinated leaders of the Spartacist League], and a twelve-year reign of terror against the revolution [Nazi rule, 1933-45]. A nation with a broken spine that made it its duty to break the spines of other nations. ... It remains our daily duty to mourn the fact that we belong to a people responsible for spreading the terror" (Müller 1990: 97).

At the same time, Müller is a world-class dramatist whose work has universal appeal. That appeal is not in spite of his German-ness, but precisely because of it. Germany was, after all, the crossroads of 20th Century history. It is on its soil that the cultural, political/ideological and military battles that would determine the course of the 21st Century were fought out to their bloody conclusion.

In the 19th Century, Germany gave birth to Marxism, a proposed alternative to the capitalist model of development that presented itself as more egalitarian and developmental. By the early 20th Century, Marxism (in both its social democratic and communist variants) had become a force to be reckoned with all over the globe. By the turn of the 20th Century, Germany had the largest socialist movement in the world. In the wake of the First World War—which might be understood as German ruling circles attempting to muscle their way into the colonial club, to which they had come late and were not welcome—there were no less than three failed attempts at communist revolution in Germany. Soon after, it was Germany that brought forth the most virulent and violent response to communism—Nazism. And, of course, after launching a war justified as the war against Bolshevism (known to us now as World War II), Germany became the epicenter of the Cold War, its infamous Berlin Wall the metaphor for the 40-year stand-off between the socialist East and the corporate West. Thus German history has been, in a very concrete sense, the distillation of world history in the 20th Century.

The Angel of History

For Müller dramatic literature has a complex and active relationship with history. In an interview in 1988, he said:

> In order to get rid of the nightmare of history, you first have to acknowledge its existence. You have to know about history. [Otherwise] It would come back in the old-fashioned way, as a nightmare, Hamlet's ghost. You have to analyze it first and then you can denounce it, get rid of it. Very important aspects of our history have been repressed for too long. ... I believe that the function of literature at his point is something like the liberation of the dead. ... I wanted to dig up things that had been covered by dirt and history and lies. Digging up the dead and showing them in the open (Müller 1990: 24, 67).

Elsewhere, he writes: "What we need is future and not the eternity of the present moment. We need to dig up the dead again and again, because from only them can a future be gained" (Linzer 1991: 29). By means of going back to the bones of German history, Müller hopes to insure that past crimes no longer lie dormant in guilt and repression. Yet for Müller, showing the dead "in the open" is not the same as chronicling what happened to them in the past. While some of his texts—*The Task, Cement*, the *Germania* trilogy—are set in the past, most, especially his late works, are in an indeterminable space/time in which past and present co-mingle. Although "DEAD IS DEAD," as Müller puts it in *Explosion of a Memory/Description of a Picture*, history is not (Müller 1989: 101). History, for Müller, is very much with us. It is, in a sense, the cultural air we breathe. Art, and particularly the performatory art of the theatre, does not simply record history, it completes it. The "completion," of course, is always incomplete. The artist, by giving voice to the ghosts among us invites us into new conversations with them—the dead who have given us the world in which we live—and we can't know in advance where these conversations may lead.

Müller's notion of history is closer to that of the Jewish-German gay Marxist philosopher/aesthetician Walter Benjamin (1892-1940) than to Marx or Brecht (or other Marxist aestheticians). Refusing all conceptions of closedness, history for Benjamin is something of an open door through which walk, in the words of the novelist Arundhati Roy, all "the vast, violent, circling, driving, ridiculous, insane, unfeasible, turmoil" of human experience (Roy: 21). For Benjamin, the past and present are a unity in history. (Hörnigk 1989: 128; Müller 1982: 25; Brenner 1989: 16-19). Benjamin focuses on the present, not as continued past, but as transformative/revolutionary, that is, as the creation of possibilities by which the subject becomes historically active (Haas/Sellner). He contends that the concept of history as a continuum of always-the-same must be exploded. The revolutionary artist is one who blasts open the continuum of history (Benjamin 1969: 263). This explosion is simultaneously destructive and constructive, because the past is the object of a construction whose perspective remains the present. All historical moments have played an equally important role in the configuration of this present. What they share in common is that they are unfinished processes active in universal human history (Brenner 1986: 8-11).

Benjamin's metaphor for history is based on a painting, "Angelus Novus," by Paul Klee, which Benjamin describes in his 1940 essay, "Theses on the Philosophy of History":

> [It] shows an angel who looking as though he is about to move away from something he is fixedly contemplating. His eyes are staring, his mouth is open, his wings spread. This is how one pictures the angel of history. His face is turned toward the past. Where we preceive a chain of events, he sees on single catastrophe which keeps piling wreckage upon wreckage and hurls it in front of his feet. The angel would like to stay, awaken the dead, and make whole what has been smashed. But a storm is blowing from Paradise; it has got caught in his wings with such violence that the angel can no longer close them. The storm irresistibly propels him into the future to which his back is turned, while the pile of debris before him grows skyward. The storm is what we call progress. (Benjamin, 1969: 257-258).

It is significant that Benjamin has his metaphor for history—the "Angelus Novus," the Angel of History—gazing towards the past, not the future. For Benjamin, history flashes up in spurts, like a series of distinct photo slides. These moments of history encapsulate as *pars pro toto* all of history, which can only be grasped in the appearances of "flashes." With Müller, as with Benjamin, progress is not located in a closed, cause-and-effect, linear conception of history, but in the activity of the conscious and creative historical subject. To articulate the past historically does not mean to recognize it "the way it really was." It means to "seize hold of a memory as it flashes up at a moment of in danger." According to Benjamin, within the work of art, taking place in the presence of now, time stands still in isolated moments of shock or fragmentation in which past and present explosively converge. (Benjamin, 1969: 255) Although he died long before Müller ever put pen to paper, there is no better description of history as an active player in Müller's plays.

Müller does not explain why things happen, he confronts his audiences with statements, montaged images and scenes, juxtaposed to de-mystify history. In destroying the act of story-telling—the explosion of the temporal continuum and its causal connections—he hopes to take away the horror of the unchangeable. History is not an abstraction; it is not over or other than human beings living their lives. The course of history lies solely in the course of life-events, as history made by people (Marx and Engels 1984: 42).

With his aesthetic method, Müller disturbs the orthodox Marxist concept of history by undercutting its sense-making faculty. His plays are embedded in an experiential space no longer governed by the promised redemption of Marxist ideology. Müller's plays do not teach lessons; they instigate experiences. Text presented in the theatre is a proposal for the audience to write its own performance text, its own aesthetic and historical experiment.

Explosive Convergence

The entirety of Müller's oeuvre could be analyzed in terms of the activistic relationship he proposes between ever-present/ever-incomplete history and art. The dynamic completion of German history through dramatic literature was Müller's self-proclaimed artistic and political task. As he put it:

> I don't want to preserve the German nation. I'm glad that it's dying. My problem is not the nation, but the memory. That's my work, this is one of its functions. I'm a German author, I'm writing in German and German literature is one of the greatest, I am sure about that. So you have to finish it. ... I can preserve the German experience. The German experience is very important. Maybe not for the Germans, but for the others to know what was this crazy nation that did all these crazy things. (Müller 1990: 86, 88)

Müller's oeuvre—ranging from the production plays of the 1950s to the synthetic fragments of his mature years—is an on-going wrestling match with German (and German-as-world) history. To examine all of Müller's texts from this perspective would take a book-length study. What I can do here is briefly sketch some of the ways in which the historic failure/catastrophe that Müller considered crucial to all 20th Century history—the defeat of the German communist revolution of 1919—flashes up again and again in his texts. It is this historic turning point that "keeps piling wreckage upon wreckage" at the feet of the Angel of History in Müller's work.

I will sidestep those texts that deal directly/obviously with German history; *Germania Death in Berlin* (1971), *The Battle* (1974), *The Road of Tanks* (1988), and *Germania 3 Ghosts at Dead Man* (1995). Since they are explicitly *about* German history, there is less to unpack. My point here is that even those plays that are not specifically German history plays, are, in their own ways, "a cancer walk through German history."

Müller's earliest produced plays *The Scab* (1956) and *The Correction* (1957) were "production plays," a genre favored by the government of the GDR in the 1950s. These were plays meant to motivate the population to work harder and increase production in order to speed the growth of socialism. Yet even here, at his formally most undeveloped, when still writing to the confining strictures of propaganda and a near-contemporary setting, his characters—industrial workers, managers and engineers—embody the "civil war" of German history as it was fought out in the early years of the GDR. Former concentration camp prisoners and former Nazis find themselves forced to work together to rebuild Germany's industrial base.

In *The Correction*, for example, Bremer, the foreman of a construction site, a communist since 1918 who spent 12 years in the camps, is forced to apologize to an engineer, a former Nazi, who he mistakenly accused of shoddy work. The new communist government needs the old Nazi's know-how and skill. As the Party Secretary tells Bremer, "Socialism isn't built with socialists only, not here and not elsewhere, and here least of all." (Müller, 2001: 32) Nothing is clean or clear cut; the German "civil war" is messy, contradictory, protracted, bloody and full of betrayal. Even in his first plays, which stylistically and dramaturgically echo Bertolt Brecht and conform to most, if not all, of the conventions of the production play, Müller is already finding ways to dig up the dead. In a 1988 interview he said of *The Scab*, "...my first published play, was very much an archeological work." The archaeologist Müller is digging up the mortal enemies of German communism and German fascism in the context of what appears to be the first victory of communism in its birthplace. "Maybe the flesh is rotten," he continued, "but they had dreams, problems, ideas that haven't decomposed in the same way." (Müller 1990: 67)

In addition to the aforementioned plays that deal directly with German history, two of Müller's major works, *Cement* (1972) and *The Task* (1979), are set in earlier historic periods, *Cement* in the Soviet Union of the 1920s and *The Task* in 18th Century Jamaica. Yet at the core of each the failure of the German revolution "flares up in danger."

In *Cement*, an adaptation of Fyodor Gladkov's 1925 novel of the same name, the stillborn German revolution and its repercussions for world history, "flares up" in the context of characters attempting to consolidate the Russian Revolution. *Cement* was the first Soviet novel to depict the struggles of the working class to rebuild Russia after the Civil War. A little less than half way into Müller's version, the communists, facing resistance to the revolution from the peasants, set up the New Economic Policy, allowing for the limited reintroduction of capitalist economic relations. Müller, in an interview, describes what comes next:

> At this point there's a short dialogue between two [communist] functionaries. "How is the revolution in Germany?" the first one asks, and the other: "There is no more revolution in Germany." Then he looks up and says: "Stars." "When I'm dead," the other replies, "I won't have to see them anymore." This is a dead point, an endpoint of the Soviet revolution and the start of the zombies' phase. But it was not the end of the play. (Müller 1990: 78)

Not the end of the play, and certainly not the end of the Russian experiment, which would not collapse for another 60 years.

The Jamaican revolution, like the German, never happened. In *The Task*—drawing on a 1958 poem, "THEME OF A.S.," and inspired by the 1961 novel, *The Light in the Gallows* (*Das Licht auf dem Galgen*) by Anna Seghers—three emissaries of the French People's Convention arrive in the English colony of Jamaica to organize a slave uprising. As their organizing work begins to take hold, word reaches them that Napoleon has seized power and is negotiating peace with the English. A revolution in Jamaica would no longer serve French national interest so the revolution in Jamaica must be called off.

Like the German uprising of 1919, the Jamaican revolution is stillborn. Given the collapse of their historic task, the three would-be revolutionaries—one the son of Jamaican slave owners, the second a French peasant, and the third a Black former slave liberated by the French Revolution—face very different options. Debuisson, the son of a slave owner, can return to his privilege, while the peasant and particularly the slave will face continued slavery and/or death. As Debuisson says to the former slave Sasportas, "I want my piece of the cake of the world. I will cut myself my piece from the hunger of the world. You, you don't own a knife." (Müller 1984: 99)

In terms of setting, characters, etc. *The Task* is perhaps Müller's least German play. Yet the grim challenge of how to live with defeat—with, perhaps, even, hopelessness—was very much the German progressive's challenge in the 20th Century. Debuisson's line to Sasportas echoes the lines of the Old Man in *Germania Death in Berlin* when describing the Spartacist Uprising to a young boy:

> ...
> The bigwigs in the palace straddled chairs
> And voted Karl and Rosa to the wall.
> We smashed the guns against the curbstones
> Crept back into the holes we lived in and
> Rolled up again the sky of our hopes.
> [Müller 1989: 46-47]

Thus the memory of the defeated German revolution "flashes up" throughout Müller's work, clashing with many theatrical settings and presents. In a speech delivered on the occasion of receiving the renowed Mülheimer Theaterpreisces for *Germania Death in Berlin*, Müller said, "My hope is for a world in which a play such as *Germania Death in Berlin* can no longer be written because reality no longer offers up material for it" (Hörnigk and Müller 1989: 101).

It is in Müller's later work that these clashes are clearest, that they, in fact, become the dramatic action. In texts such as *Hamletmachine* (1978), *Despoiled Shore/Medeamaterial/Landscape with Argonauts* (1982), and *Explosion of a Memory/Description of a Picture* (1984) Müller does away with the constraints of plot and, in some cases, character. This allows him to bring images, lines, and literary, political and historical references into direct conflict with each other, unrestrained by the distracting layers of theatrical convention. In his later work Müller clears the stage of the niceties of narrative and psychological clutter and allows the wreckage of history to pile up directly in front of us. While each of Müller's later works deals with very specific political-cultural concerns, the thread that runs through them all is the on-going conflictedness and stasis of the Cold War, the "frozen storm" that he refers to at the end of *Explosion of a Memory* (Müller 1989: 102).

In one of Müller's last works for the stage, *Mommsen's Block* (1993), he grapples for the first, and only, time with capitalist ascendancy throughout Germany (and Europe). It was certainly, from his point of view, another defeat—at best a continuation of the German "civil war" under new circumstances, at worst it meant the 20th Century's dreams of egalitarian revolution reduced to historical insignificance. As he put it in the text:

THE GREAT OCTOBER OF THE WORKING CLASS-extolled
Voluntarily with hope or in a twofold stranglehold

By too many and even after their throats had been cut–
Was a summer storm in the World Bank's shadow
A dance of gnats above the graves of Tartars
WHERE THE DEAD ONES WAIT
FOR THE EARTHQUAKES TO COME
(Müller: 2001: 128)

Müller was, in a very real sense, trapped by the fall of the Wall in a new political, cultural and economic reality, and found himself struggling to write in this new historical situation. *Mommsen's Block* ostensively addresses the 19th Century historian Theodor Mommsen's inability to complete his history of the Roman Empire. Müller also writes of his own writer's block when faced with the apparent defeat of socialism. He describes himself sitting in a restaurant beside, "Two heroes of the new time … /Zombies of capital brokers and traders/And as I listened to their dialogue greedy/To feed my disgust with the Here and Now." After quoting their conversation in some detail he despairs, "Animal sounds Who would write that down/With passion Hate is a waste Contempt an empty exercise/For the first time I understand your writer's block/Comrade Professor facing the Roman age of the Caesars" (Müller: 2001:128-129). In this late text, Müller, the political human being and the playwright, finds himself to be a piece of the historic wreckage with which he has populated his texts.

History on a new stage

What follows is offered in the spirit of an epilogue (with the potential to become a prologue).

In his work from *Hamletmachine* on, Müller, while he continued to view his work as an attempt to "preserve the German experience," increasingly recognized (and welcomed) the shift of historical motion to the impoverished South, to what, during much of the Cold War, was referred to as the Third World. As early as *The Task* Müller has his only specifically black character, the former slave Sasportas, say:

> The Theatre of the white Revolution is over […] Slaves have no home […] as long as there are masters and slaves, we won't be released from our task […] on the gallows I will know that my accomplices are the negroes of all races whose number grows with every minute that you spend at your slaveholder's trough […] When the living can no longer fight, the dead will. With every heartbeat of the revolution flesh grows back on their bones […] I—that is Africa. I—that is Asia. The two Americas—that is I. (Müller 1984: 93, 97, 100)

In 1990, Müller spoke of the peace that had reigned in Europe from 1945 until the collapse of communism as a false peace that covered over the endless war being waged in the rest of the world.

> When we speak of peace in Europe we speak of peace in war. A war on at least three continents. Peace in Europe has never been anything else. Just as fascism was a red hot episode in the century-long capitalistic world war, a geographic lapsus, genocide in Europe instead of in South America, Africa and Asia where it was and is the norm. (Müller 1990: 229)

This war takes many forms but is, in Müller's estimation, essentially a class war (and, I might add, a race and gender war between "masters and slaves)—the continuation and expansion of the battles that ripped Germany and Europe apart in the mid-20th Century. While the Black Revolution anticipated in *The Task* may look very different from the revolutions fought and lost in Central and Eastern Europe in the 20th century, this shift away from the failures of Germany and Europe was a source of inspiration, if not hope, for Müller. As he put it, "I'm waiting for the Third World [...] It is the great threat for the West and the great hope for our side" (Müller 1990: 33).

Nor did it escape Müller that the so-called Third World was beginning to transform the so-called First World.

> For the moment everyone seems to agree that communism has failed, but one could also say that communism has thrown off its political-ideological costume and appears naked before our eyes in the shape of immigrants. The problem remains: poverty verses wealth. (Linzer 1991: 12)

Müller's life's work of completing German history on stage, thus, by his own account, may be but a preamble to a whole new storm blowing from Paradise.

Work Cited

Benjamin, Walter (1969). "Theses on the Philosophy of History." *Illuminations*. Trans. Harry Zohn. New York: Schocken Books, pp. 253-264.

Brenner, Eva (1986). Notes on the production of Robert Wilson's HAMLETMACHINE. New York. July 1986. Unpublished.

—. (1987). Conversation with Heiner Muller. East Berlin, October 10. Unpublished.

—. (1989). "Crossroads Berlin." *Stono*, Vol. I, No. 1, May/June: 16-19.

Haas, Aziza and Sellner, Angela (1984). "Die Dramaturgie der Geschichte in den Stucken Heiner Muller's von *Zement* bis *Der Auftrag*. ["The Dramaturgy of History in the plays of Heiner Müller from *Cement* to *The Task*."] Unpublished term paper at the University of Cologne. Excerpts translated by Eva Brenner.

Hörnigk, Frank and Müller, Heiner (1989). *Heiner Müller Material: Text und Kommentare*. Göttingen: Steidl Verlag, p. 101

Linzer, Martin (1991). "... rückwarts in die Gegenwart." Zu Heiner Müller's Mauser Projekt am Deutschen Theater. Gespraech mit Heiner Müller vor der Mauser Premiere am Deutschen Theater. Theater der Zeit. November Sonderheft.

Marx, Karl and Engels, Frederick (1984). *The German Ideology*. New York: International Publishers.

Müller, Heiner (1982). *Rotwelsch*. Berlin: Merve Verlag.

—. (1984). *Hamletmachine and Other Texts for the Stage*. Ed. and trans. Carl Weber. New York: Performing Arts Journal Publications.

—. (1989). *Explosion of a Memory*. Ed. and trans. Carl Weber. New York: Performing Arts Journal Publications.

—. (1990). *Germania*. Ed. Sylveré Lotringer. Trans. Bernard and Caroline Schütze. New York: Semiotext(e), 1990.

—. (2001). *A Heiner Müller Reader*. Ed. and trans. Carl Weber. Baltimore and London: The John Hopkins University Press.

Roy, Arundhati (1998). *The God of Small Things*. New York: Harper Perennial.

Schödel, Helmut (1993). "Das Todeskapitel." *Die Zeit* Nr. 41. October 8: 57.

PART II

DIGGING UP THE DEAD: MÜLLER'S USE AND TRANSFORMATION OF THE WESTERN TRADITION

"What we need is future and not the eternity of the present. We need to dig up the dead again and again, because only from them can the future be gained."
—Heiner Müller, 1991

INTRODUCTION

All artists, of course, build on those who came before. Nothing comes from nothing, and as the American folk singer Pete Seeger is fond of saying, "Plagiarism is the basis of all culture." Indeed, a good working definition of creativity might well be the ability to take what is and reorganize it into something new.

While all artists build with what has come before, in the modernist tradition the building material from the past tends to be hidden out of sight, in the foundation and beams of the new structure. The emphasis, the aesthetic gaze, is on what the individuated artist has added to the mix. For Müller, in his later work at least, nothing is hidden. His "synthetic fragments" might be understood as piles of rubble. Scraps of characters, sentences, images, ideas, echoes of events from the world's cultural and historical legacy juxtaposed and stacked together in untried and disturbing combinations. Müller called this "digging up the dead," and it is essential, as many of the essays in this collection argue, to understanding both his aesthetic and his politic.

In her chapter, "A Cancer Walk Through German History" in the first section of this book, Eva Brenner shows how the synthetic fragment is tied to Müller's understanding of history (and politics). In this section, our contributors take very specific looks at Müller's best-known synthetic fragment, *Hamletmachine* (1979). While virtually all of Müller's texts, from *Cement* (1972) on, are rich in allusion, quotation, paraphrase and historical reference, *Hamletmachine* consists of little else. It is, to borrow a word that Magda Romanska in her chapter uses to describe the play's Ophelia character, a "cipher" of literary and historical allusion.

Hamletmachine is also, as Roger Bechtel argues in his chapter, "*Hamletmachine* and Allegorical History," an allegory. Starting from the premise that allegory is "the formal impulse motivating much postmodern aesthetic production," he approaches *Hamletmachine* as an allegory of *Hamlet*, (the play, not the character). Drawing, as Brenner did, on the work of Walter Benjamin, Bechtel makes a case for the subversive nature of allegory. "Unlike the symbol, which *is* the idea it also transfigures," he writes, "the allegory says one thing and means another." In looking at *Hamletmachine* in this way, Bechtel gives us another approach not only to this particular text but also to all of Müller's later work, and perhaps to other contemporary texts for the stage being labeled—vaguely and tentatively—postmodern.

Magda Romanska in her chapter, "Opheliamachine: Gender, Ethics and Representation in Heiner Müller's *Hamletmachine*," provides a brilliant literary and political analysis of Müller's use of the character of Ophelia in his signature play. She traces German culture's use of Ophelia (and Hamlet) from the late 18th Century to the present—in drama, poetry, the fine arts, medicine and psychology—and explores how the various images, articulations, and manifestations of Ophelia and Hamlet fed into to the coming-into-being German nationalism of the 19th Century and, at the same time, contributed to the specifics of gender identity within German culture. In so doing, Romanska traces the cross-fertilization (if you will) between the shaping of gender and the shaping of nation in Germany. Showing how Müller made use of all this cultural baggage, Romanska provides a non-polemical look at Müller's own conflicted relationship—in *Hamletmachine* and elsewhere—to the radical feminism of the late 20th Century. In so doing, she provides not only an erudite look at Müller's digging up of the dead in *Hamletmachine*, but points forward to this volume's third section which explores Müller in relation to the unfolding political culture of the 21st Century.

Work Cited

Linzer, Martin. "… ruckwarts in die gegenwart. Zu Heiner Müller's *Mauser* Projekt am Deutschen Theater. Gespraech mit Heiner Müller. Theater der Zeit. November Sonderheft 1991: 10. Translation by Eva Brenner, quoted in "HAMLETMACHINE Onstage: A Critical Analysis of Heiner Müller's Play in Production." DAI 55 (1994): 14. New York University.

CHAPTER FOUR

HAMLETMACHINE AND ALLEGORICAL HISTORY

ROGER BECHTEL

The photograph is both amusing and compelling: Heiner Müller in 1990, can of spray paint in hand, graffiti-ing the word "**CON**STRUCTIV" on one of this century's most notorious constructions, the Berlin Wall (Kalb 1996: 71). Writing literally *on* history, choosing as a medium the material remains of a now-sedimented historical moment—the Cold War as corpse—is not a novel gesture for Heiner Müller, and this playful bit of vandalism is not unlike the strategy he brings to some of his most penetrating theatre pieces—particularly *Hamletmachine*. Like writing on the Berlin Wall, there is a historical double-consciousness at work in *Hamletmachine* insofar as it, too, is a material remains, Shakespeare's *Hamlet* reduced to ruins by the melancholy gaze of the late Twentieth Century.

Doubleness, of course, is a defining feature of the allegorical mode, and despite the fall from favor it suffered at the hands of the Romantics, allegory has experienced a revival of late as the formal impulse motivating much postmodern aesthetic production. The theoretical inspiration for its renaissance is indisputably Walter Benjamin, primarily his early *The Origin of German Tragic Drama*, in which he illuminates the capacity for certain modes of allegory to turn language into material fragments. Literally "objectifying" language in this way endows allegory with its own unique parabolic historicity. Captured in the uncanny life of ruins, allegorical history has the unique ability to bend our historically retrospective gaze prospectively—a phenomenon that I want to address here in relation to both the text of *Hamletmachine* and its particular staging by Robert Wilson—an American production, it should be noted, of what Müller called his "most American play" (qtd. in Brenner: 550).

The Allegorical Impulse

For Benjamin, allegory was distinguished by its unique engagement with two central aesthetic categories: time and totality—categories which writers and critics from Goethe to Yeats have marshaled against allegory and in favor of the symbol. In the symbol, time is collapsed into a transcendent moment, in which the essence of the artwork, the marriage of form and content that constitutes its totality, is manifested in a single one of its elements: the transient image. Allegory, conversely, is durational in nature and in disposition: time becomes its defining feature as well as its object. Instead of provoking metaphysical insight through what Benjamin calls a "mystical instant" (Benjamin: 165), allegory accumulates meaning through a process of accretion. "The distinction between the two modes is therefore to be sought in the momentariness which allegory lacks," Benjamin notes, "There [in the symbol] we have momentary totality; here [in the allegory] we have progression in a series of moments" (Benjamin: 165).

If the defining differences between symbol and allegory went only this far, we might still readily understand postmodernism's recuperation of allegory, the symbolic being immediately suspect in its metaphysical claims to totality, transcendence, and essence. Allegory is "the privileged mode of our own life," writes Fredric Jameson, "a clumsy deciphering of meaning from moment to moment, the painful attempt to restore a continuity to heterogeneous, disconnected events" (Jameson 1971: 72). The aesthetic claims of allegory, however, extend much further, yet they all grow out of the subversive potential inseparable from its very nature: unlike the symbol, which *is* the idea it also transfigures, the allegory says one thing and means another. In his seminal study on allegory, Angus Fletcher observes, "[Allegory] destroys the normal expectation we have about language, that our words 'mean what they say.'...Pushed to the extreme, this ironic usage would subvert language itself..." (Fletcher: 2).

In addition to the semantic implications of this revelation—and this is perhaps the pivotal point—under the "melancholy gaze" of the allegorist, language is splintered into linguistic scraps that can become material objects in their own right—what Benjamin called "amorphous fragment[s]" (Benjamin: 176). He writes:

> In the anagrams, the onomatopoeic phrases, and many other examples of linguistic virtuosity, word, syllable and sound are emancipated from any context of traditional meaning and are flaunted as objects which can be exploited for allegorical purposes (Benjamin: 207).

Stripped of its semantic flesh by the allegorist—whether of the *Trauerspiel* or of *Hamletmachine*—what is left of language is its scattered bones. Thus language "lives" only when it remains the seemingly transparent purveyor of meaning. When meaning-making loses this transparency, however, when we are confronted with language as an arbitrary, combinatory, and, importantly, *durational* medium—as allegory—language takes the first step not only toward objectification but toward ossification. And in this process, as creatures of language, we apprehend our own inevitable petrifaction. This is language as ruins, embedded in which is nothing less than the historicity of the world. Benjamin describes this dynamic as follows:

> ...in allegory the observer is confronted with the *facies hippocratia* of history as a petrified, primordial landscape. Everything about history that, from the very beginning, has been untimely, sorrowful, unsuccessful, is expressed in a face—or rather in a death's head. And although such a thing lacks all "symbolic" freedom of expression, all classical proportion, all humanity—nevertheless, this is the form in which man's subjection to nature is most obvious... (Benjamin: 166).

Death's presence makes immediately apprehensible the dialectical relationship between nature and history, between the ineluctable force of decline of the former and the factitiousness of the latter. This is the power of ruins: to force a retrospective gaze toward some lost origin, however imaginary; then elliptically to lead that gaze through the ages of decay that has rendered this thing, this object, merely the remnants of time; and finally to project ourselves toward the imaginary but inevitable future. In this experience of complex seeing there is, as Benjamin would have it, a momentary cessation of the dialectic of history, allowing insight as well into the mutability of history and our "weak messianic" power over it — which, weak precisely because of the impossibility of transcendence, embraces allegory as one of its most formidable weapons.

Hamletmachine: Allegorical Mode

Heiner Müller's engagement with history as a playwright can be seen as a continual struggle against the historical abyss on both sides of the Wall. Like Brecht, Müller tried different aesthetic gambits throughout his oeuvre, but his continued attack on historical representation is marked most visibly and consistently by a strategy of radical negation, one ultimately more Adornian than Brechtian. Such radical negation is not incompatible with the allegorical mode and its other effects—in fact, just the opposite—and *Hamletmachine* is nothing less than an allegory of *Hamlet*, that is, not the character, but the play as a cultural artifact. Broken down, burnt out, *Hamlet*'s dramatic machinery grinds to a halt in *Hamletmachine*, the play's story of transcendence through action rejected by an anti-hero anti-Hamlet who no longer believes in transcendence or the efficacy of action, or, for that matter, stories. *Hamletmachine* may retain the five-act skeleton of Shakespeare's play, may indeed tell a story, but it is the story of the failure of stories: the failure of Hamlet to act, the failure of Ophelia's revolt. There is no climax, no action per se, no dialogue. Both on the level of motif and the level of structure, *Hamletmachine* enacts, as both Jonathan Kalb and Aileen Teraoka claim, the death of drama—or, more specifically, the failure of traditional dramatic form either to express or to challenge the world. That this inadequacy reflects the death of history—or, in other words, that the death of history and the death of drama are allegorically coterminous here—is addressed by Müller: "With my last play *Hamletmachine* that's come to an end. No substance for dialogue exists anymore because there is no history" (qtd. in Kalb, 2001: 107).

At the same time, it is not enough for *Hamletmachine* simply to announce or enact the death of drama, even if it whistles past the gravesite. This is precisely the problem with a strictly Artaudian reading of the play (a favorite of recent American critics): it may address the problem of drama, which is to say the problem of representation, but it does not address the problem of history. Understood as an allegory in Benjaminian mode, however, the play's vortex becomes history itself, which it attempts to recuperate through its shrapnel-ridden and shattered allegorical construction. Generically, *Hamletmachine* may announce the death of drama, but its historical power derives from a more specific obituary: the death of *Hamlet*. *Hamlet* is the ghost in the *Hamletmachine*, or rather the corpse in its coffin, for its exposed outmodedness marks it with the presence of death, disabuses it of any transcendental spirit, and exorcises its importunate specter. Its inertness gives it a certain uncanny power, the ability to transfix our gaze in the same way that a human corpse simultaneously repulses and attracts it. It is as a *memento mori* that *Hamlet* achieves one of its most potent performances: if, living, it was always an associative stand-in for the achievement of Western culture; in death it exposes the cancer that devours that culture from within. As Benjamin claims, the human corpse compels us to question our own "biographical historicity," endows us with a sense of both our own mortality and temporality; here, the corpse of *Hamlet* enlarges that apprehension to encompass the entirety of Western history. This is the

historical nature and natural history of *Hamlet* embodied—or entombed—
in *Hamletmachine*.

For *Hamletmachine* to compel our historical gaze, however, it must
successfully perform its own feat of allegorical alchemy, turning words
into objects that pile one after another until they accumulate in the form of
a ruins. In this respect, Benjamin's observation of the material density
accruing to the language of the *Trauerspiel* is equally applicable to
Hamletmachine: it, too, is "heavy with material display" (Benjamin: 200).
Most visually striking in *Hamletmachine* are the interpolations of lines of
all-capitalized text. These lines are often quotations or bastardizations, but
not always, and they usually contribute to the thematic/substantive flow of
the text, but sometimes disrupt it. For example:

> Ich legte mich auf den Boden und hörte die Welt ihre Runden drehn im
> Gleichschritt der Verwesung.
> I'M GOOD HAMLET GI'ME A CAUSE FOR GRIEF
> (Müller 2001, 4: 545)

Quoting the original text without translation illuminates another
striking attribute: many of these capitalized lines are not in German but in
English, which endows them with a hieroglyphic intensity for non-
speakers.

The text also alternates between blocks of prose and sections of poetry;
in the latter, the lines are often systematically truncated or elongated and
arranged to form patterns on the page. One section creates its own visual
vortex or entropy by progressively shortening its lines – here are the first
and last:

> Geh ich durch Strassen Kaufhallen Gesichter.
> …
> Heil COCA COLA.
> (Müller 2001, 4: 552)

Müller also plays visually with individual words, sometimes eliding
them—"HoratioPolonius" (Müller 2001, 4: 546)—sometimes capitalizing
them—"Scarred by the subsistence battle Poverty" (Müller 2002, 4:
552)—and sometimes using grammatical devices to disrupt them—"at
one/with my undivided self" (Müller 2001, 4: 551). Finally, the stage
directions appear in italics, which is not in itself unusual. But given that
the third act, the "SCHERZO," is almost wholly stage directions, the
forward thrust of the italicized characters captures the whirling action of

the scene in its whirling words, creating at the center of the play text another kind of visual vortex.

While each of these effects serves in its own right to imbue the language with material density, they also contribute to its fragmentary quality. For Benjamin, this quality plays a significant part in the objectification of the language: "In its individual parts fragmented language has ceased merely to serve the process of communication, but as new-born object acquires a dignity equal to that of gods, rivers, virtues and similar natural forms which fuse into the allegorical" (Benjamin: 208). Implied here is a recursive quality between materiality and fragmentation: it is as if words freeze into objects upon hitting the chill air of in-significance. Or to put it differently, rendering words into objects necessitates breaking them, literally, out of the ethereal flow of signification.

Hamletmachine's allegorical quality is intensified by another related attribute which was absent in the *Trauerspiel* as such: the quotation of or reference to other literary or philosophic works. As Kalb points out, the play is "[p]acked with quotations and paraphrases from Eliot, cummings, Hölderlin, Marx, Benjamin, Artaud, Sartre, Warhol, Shakespeare, the Bible, Müller himself, and others, often strung together without connecting text..." (Kalb 2001: 108). The myriad quotes themselves crystallize as fragments, embedded in and splintering the *Hamletmachine* text even further. Taken out of their original context and placed in another, the quotes become literally object-ified. In other words, these quotes are distinguishable not only as language fragments but as foreign objects, bits of shrapnel in the already broken body of the text.

An American Production

The allegorical effect Benjamin describes, as he recognizes, is one most readily realized on the page, for it is there that we come into direct contact with the written word. How such an effect translates to the stage is more problematic, and on this point Benjamin remains equivocal. Yet in his insistence that the relationship between written and spoken language is dialectical, that they "confront each other in tense polarity," he intimates that the allegorical effect of writing is not necessarily lost in performance (Benjamin: 201). The challenge of *Hamletmachine* then is to find a staging strategy compatible with its uniquely postmodern allegorical attitude. The magnitude of this challenge, however, is not to be underestimated. By offering "resistance to the theatre," the task Müller set for dramatic literature (Müller 1989: 160), *Hamletmachine* does not

necessarily force unconventional productions as much as it deflates
conventional ones; critic and director Andrzej Wirth calls it a "theatrically
impossible text (as many prior attempts at staging seem to have proven)"
(Wirth: 215). The exception that Wirth marshals to prove the rule,
however, is Robert Wilson's production, one of the most critically
successful stagings of the play to date. What has united the various critics
in their praise of Wilson's *Hamletmachine* is the crowbar separation it
forces between text and mise-en-scène, allowing them both to run as if on
disjunct but parallel tracks. This is precisely the aspect of the production
that I want to address, but from the perspective that such a strategy
maintains the text's allegorical impact in the context of theatrical
performance.

Wilson's production is well known to Müller scholars and admirers, so
it needn't be recounted in detail here. With regard to Wilson's process,
however, it is worth noting that Wilson developed his idiosyncratic
choreography before layering the *Hamletmachine* text onto it. Moreover,
the choreography was supposedly created without specific regard to the
text. As he describes it:

> I came to Berlin to see Heiner before I went to New York, and I asked
> what he could tell me about it. He said, "No, do what you want with it."
> "Help me a little." (*laughs*) He said, "It shouldn't be longer than fifty
> minutes." I said, "Okay." Then I went to New York and worked for ten
> days—I only had three weeks—and staged all the action and movements
> without thinking about the text, and then laid the text over the movements,
> and then started to fit the movements to the text. (qtd. in Hentschker 62;
> translation mine)

While Wilson's production obviously reflects some level of
engagement with the text—its clocklike circularity and choreographic
inertia a perfect reflection of historical stasis, pungently flavored by the
boozy disappointment of the Peggy Lee soundtrack—no effort was made
either to adduce or delimit meaning through an active process of
illustration. The stringent partitioning of text and mise-en-scène eschews
mimesis, and instead forces the language and its visual and aural context
"to confront each other in tense polarity," to reiterate Benjamin's phrase,
without submitting either to dialectical sublation. Pushing his strategy
even further, Wilson was at pains to dissociate the text from the
performances as well. To this end, he found the undergraduate actors to
be ideal performers: trained but not experienced, and willing to accept his

direction at face value. He emphasized that the actors should not imbue the lines with emotion, but speak them neutrally.

Wilson's overarching strategy of disengaging language from mise-en-scène was far from accidental. If there is any doubt that he was deliberately seeking a means of staging that would allow the text of *Hamletmachine* to retain its unique material density, it should be eliminated by his referring to Müller's language as "rocks": "I am free to imagine where I will place these rocks, these stones of words into [my] landscapes. It is a little bit as if one was to make a silent movie and a radio play at the same time" (qtd. in Brenner: 495). Müller, too, commented on this aspect of Wilson's approach: "Bob treats a text like a piece of furniture. He doesn't try to break it up or break it open or try to get information out of it or meaning or emotion. It's just a thing. That's what I like about his way because a text can stand for itself" (qtd. in Shyer: 123). Yet Wilson does more than simply create the relational conditions that allow the language its "thing-ness," he gives the language the *time* necessary to exist as an object. Here Wilson's notorious slowness is incorporated to particularly good effect: the "fifty minutes" running time advised by Müller stretches to two and a half hours in Wilson's production, the tempo of the recited words and, perhaps even more importantly, their solitary isolation within a prolonged rhythm of silence and sound imbues them with a kind of ontological gravity. Their meaning becomes secondary to their existence; like planets floating slowly through empty space, their discovery as bodies precedes and takes precedence over their decipherment as signs.

If Wilson's *Hamletmachine* exemplifies one formal approach to staging this type of allegory, it operates effectively on the level of motif as well. Without straitjacketing the text into some necessarily delimited interpretive meaning, Wilson nevertheless apprehends the idea of historical stasis—or perhaps simply understands the stasis inherent in the text—and embodies this idea in the structure of his staging. The mechanistic aspect of *Hamletmachine* becomes the production's central conceit: the stage itself as machine, rotating and repeating *ad infinitum*. In fact, Wilson's earliest design concept centered on the image of a clock: "In the case of *Hamletmachine* ... I knew I was going to build a play out of this thin table that was turning like a machine or clock in a room" (qtd. in Brenner: 440). The semiotics of the mise-en-scène combine in this regard to signal a strange historical space: the reflexive indeterminacy of place refuses historicity, while at the same time the Victorian, 1940s, and contemporary dress embody it, creating a temporally void dumping ground for the refuse of historical fashion, the junkyard at the end of history.

Wilson's theatrical *longue durée* expands this effect: as his time/machine drags relentlessly on, we experience time viscerally, while apprehending the action of the machine—i.e., history—as repetitive stasis. The text might alter from act to act, along with the spectators' shifting perspective on the (in)action, but the eternal return of each and every gesture and attitude finally betrays the perception of change as mere illusion. In this production, as in all instances of Benjaminian allegory, time flies, but the feet of history are stuck in the mire.

Fredric Jameson famously calls the postmodern condition "an attempt to think the present historically in an age that has forgotten how to think historically in the first place" (Jameson 1991: ix). If this is accurate, it is surely epitomized by American culture, which has always had a historical blind spot. It is perhaps then no accident that Wilson's American production of this German play has been widely recognized as perhaps the most successful to date, or that *Hamletmachine* has become canonized as the first postmodern "classic" (if that oxymoronic designation can be used) in W.B. Worthen's *Wadsworth Anthology of Drama*, or that it seems to be eking out a consistent place in the American repertory. Cursory Internet research reveals fifteen recent university productions and six done at small urban theatres across the country. The prompt for this interest might be found in the text itself, as Müller notes: "When I wrote HAMLETMACHINE, after translating Shakespeare's *Hamlet* for a theater in East Berlin, it turned out to be my most American play, quoting T.S. Eliot, Andy Warhol, Coca Cola, Ezra Pound, and Susan Atkins. It may be read as a pamphlet against the illusion that one can stay innocent in this our world" (qtd. in Brenner: 550). The innocent always end up with blood on their hands, as Müller elsewhere acknowledges, and if the play is his "most American," it is as an allegory of America's blindness to its own bloodstained history.

Yet if *Hamletmachine* has insinuated itself into the psyche of American theatre artists, it is likely attributable not specifically to an American urge to awaken its own repressed history, but to the play's broader disabuse of the centuries-old Enlightenment claim that history is finally redemptive. Wilson's use of Peggy Lee is trenchant: *Is* that all there is? Is this really where history has finally left us? If the American resurgence of interest in *Hamletmachine* goes beyond mere canonical fashionmongering, surely it has something to do with its sense of historical despair, its melancholy allegorist's gaze. In the new age of empire, America can no longer maintain the conveniently self-deluding rhetoric of American innocence. Müller's suggestion that the play is a "pamphlet" against the illusion that innocence can be maintained in today's world does indeed strike at a peculiarly self-imposed American naïveté, and the spate of recent stateside revivals might be seen as reflecting a growing disillusion with such posturing, an inchoate longing to break the bonds of historical impasse everywhere reinforced in the language of American self-righteousness. But it is also precisely in its ability to embody the desire *for* history, to articulate this desire in a way foreclosed to the symbol, that the death's head of allegory transcends morbidity, for through its unique "history lesson" it can prompt a living response. "I stood on the shore and talked with the surf, BLA BLA, the ruins of Europe in back of me," Müller's Hamlet figure begins the performance (Müller 1984: 53). Through the refractive lens of allegory, this image of Europe that we cannot help but place in 1945 bends our gaze toward the future, exposing other ruins too possible to ignore.

Work Cited

Benjamin, Walter (1985). *The Origin of German Tragic Drama.* Trans. John Osborne. New York: Verso.

Brenner, Eva (1994). "HAMLETMACHINE Onstage: A Critical Analysis of Heiner Müller's Play in Production." *DAI* 55: 9. New York University.

Fletcher, Angus (1964). *Allegory: The Theory of a Symbolic Mode.* Ithaca: Cornell University Press.

Hentschker, Frank, et. al. (1988). "Be Stupid." *Explosion of a Memory Heiner Müller DDR: Ein Arbeitsbuch.* Ed. Wolfgang Storch. Berlin: Hentrich.

Jameson, Fredric (1971). *Marxism and Form.* Princeton: Princeton University Press.

—. 1991) *Postmodernism, or, the Cultural Logic of Late Capitalism.* Durham: Duke University Press.

Kalb, Jonathan (1996). "On the Becoming Death of Poor H.M." *Theater* 2:1, pp. 65-73.

—. (2001). *The Theatre of Heiner Müller.* New York: Limelight, 2001.

Müller, Heiner (1984). *Hamletmachine and Other Texts for the Stage.* Ed. and Trans. Carl Weber. New York: Performing Arts Journal Publications.

—. (1989). "Literature Must Offer Resistance to the Theatre." *The Battle.* Ed. and Trans. Carl Weber. New York: Performing Arts Journal Publications:153-172.

—. (2001). *Werke.* Ed. Frank Hörnigk. 4 vols. Frankfurt am Main: Suhrkamp Verlag.

Shyer, Laurence (1989). *Robert Wilson and His Collaborators*. New York: Theater Communications Group.

Teraoka, Arlene Akiko (1985). *The Silence of Entropy or Universal Discourse*. New York, Berne, Frankfurt am Main: Peter Lang.

Wirth, Andrzej (1995). "Heiner Müller and Robert Wilson: An Unlikely Convergence." *Heiner Müller ConTEXTS and HISTORY*. Ed. Gerhard Fisher. Tübingen: Stauffenburg Verlag.

Worthen, W.B., Ed. *The Wadsworth Anthology of Drama*. Boston: Thomson Wadsworth, 2007.

CHAPTER FIVE

OPHELIAMACHINE:
GENDER, ETHICS AND REPRESENTATION
IN HEINER MULLER'S *HAMLETMACHINE*

MAGDA ROMANSKA

Germany is Hamlet! Mute and grave,
within its gates stalks every night
entombed freedom and does wave
to those on watch who see this sight.
Then, stopping, lofty, bright in arms, she says to him, who doubts and fears:
"Avenge me, draw, throw off the charms,
for they poured poison in my ears!"

—Ferdinand Freiligrath, 1844, Quoted in Pfister, Manfred. "Germany is Hamlet: The History of a Political Interpretation," *New Comparison: A Journal of Comparative and General Literary Studies* 2 (Autumn, 1986).

1. "Germany is Hamlet" (or not):
Hamlet, Masculinity, and the German *Gestalt*

Writing *Hamletmachine* in 1977, Müller reacted to the reality of a divided Germany, to its post-war attempts at "remasculinization," as well as to the gendered history of German nationalism as it became bound to and defined by Hamlet's myth. In *Nationalism and Sexuality*, George Mosse argues that the Nineteenth-Century concept of masculinity that emerged in Germany was tinted by nationalistic undertones insofar as it entailed control over one's sexual impulses (with an exclusive emphasis on heterosexuality), manly military camaraderie, and redemptive vengeful violence toward the enemy: to be patriotic meant, foremost, to be masculine. Masculinity became the very "foundation of the nation and society" (Mosse 1985: 17); it was a matter of courage, "an outward

symbol of the inner spirit" (Mosse 1985:13).[1] The image of Hamlet as a
man of state, seeking to assert his rights and manhood through violent
revenge, became dominant trope of the 19th Century German identity
(Zimmermann 1994: 294). Following Goethe, Hegel saw Hamlet's
revenge as "ethically justified" and uncontestable (prompted by the Law of
the Father) (qtd. in Paulin 2003: 371). Eventually the motive of revenge
became quintessential to Germany's understanding of Hamlet and itself.
The late 19th Century German youth "saw in [Hamlet] the symbolic
fulfillment of their own aspirations and dreams—an aristocratic hero
who . . . successfully resolves the conflict between ideals and actions and
who fights against corruption and oppression" (Pfister 1986: 105).[2] In
Shakespeare and the German Spirit, Friedrich Gundolf suggested that
Hamlet formed the very core of Germany's national sense of self-
definition.[3] Gundolf considers *Hamlet* a national myth, like the Bible or
Homer, a "symptom and element of German *Bildung*" (Gundolf 1911:
316, 318). Describing Hamlet as a resolute avenger who overcomes his
nihilism in the name of higher ideals and eventually embraces his
masculine/patriotic obligations to kill and to die for his Father/land,
Gundolf writes a history of *Geistesgeschichte* as the self-discovery of
quintessential German-ness through the prism of Hamlet's redemptive
narrative.[4] On the eve of the World War I, this proud image of Hamlet as
heroic avenger made the play a must for every contemporary acting
company. In just the 1911–1912 theatre season alone, the *Yearbook* of The
German Shakespeare Society reported 413 different Shakespeare
productions staged throughout Germany by 178 companies; most of them
were productions of *Hamlet*.[5]

Parallel to the popularity of the avenging Hamlet that eventually
gripped turn-of-the- century Germany ran a morbid enthrallment with the
image of the drowned Ophelia. If Hamlet was a model of nationalized
masculinity obliged to die for the Father/land, she was an image of passive
femininity obliged to die for *him*. Beginning in the late nineteenth century
and continuing until World War II, the image of a drowned women (a.k.a
Ophelia) inspired an entire generation of German poets. Rimbaud's 1870
poem *Ophélie*,[6] translated into German by Karl Clammy in 1907, became
a prototype for the so-called German "water corpse poetry"
(*Wasserleichenpoesie*) of the early Twentieth Century that dominated
German sensibility.[7] The more a model of nationalized, death-driven
masculinity Hamlet turned out to be, the more popular the image of
Ophelia's corpse became. She was imagined as melancholic, idealistic,
naïve, and foremost self-destructive.

2. "Hamlet Divides in Two and Self-Destructs"

As a student of history and literature, in the 1970s Müller was aware of the role that *Hamlet* played in Germany's national consciousness. In *Hamletmachine*, he analyzes the relationship between gender, the failure of Germany's nationalist model, and the ethos of the death drive that structured the gender difference, that Hamlet and Ophelia came to embody. The title of the play itself, *Hamletmachine*, refers to the machine of German *Geistesgeschichte* that Hamlet helped to propel; it is as if it were "a shrunken head version of *Hamlet*" (Guntner and McLean 1988: 55). Following Germany's "myth of Hamlet," the play is a reflection on representation, gender relations, and totalitarian politics (Kalb 1998b: 109). Wilhem Hortmann calls it "the destruction of patriarchal myth surrounding Shakespeare's play" (Hortmann 1991: 432). In *Hamletmachine*, Hamlet's identity crisis is a crisis of masculinity defined by national identity and destroyed by the split of that identity (with the post-war separation of East and West). Shortly after the war, within the complex intersection of gender, patriarchy, and national identity, "the space of German masculinity, . . . , became one of the key places through which growing anxieties about a German male came to the forefront as the focal point of public concern and cultural resolution" (Jeffords 1998; 163–164). In both West and East, "the construction of 'German manhood' was subject to widespread ambiguities" and what follows, the idea of gender and the role of feminine within the nation-state became a political matter" (Jeffords 1998: 164). *Hamletmachine* captures this history of the deconstruction and reconstruction of Germany's national and gender identities. Thus, Müller is reacting to both the image of Hamlet that had pervaded German culture since the late Eighteenth Century, but also the morbid image of suicidal Ophelia that haunted the German sensibility. His intention was, as he put it himself, "to make Ophelia a character of equal importance" (Weber 1984: 51). Hence, Ophelia figures as both Hamlet's feminine *alter ego* and his unwitting incarnation, ignominy, and menace, his "monstrous double," to borrow a phrase from Rene Girard, "Ophelias" is framed by Hamlet's death drive, defined by and sustained by his historically German masculinity.

3. OpheliaMachine: Deconstructing the Myth

There is a general contention among theatre critics that Müller's representation of femininity in *Hamletmachine*, is at best ambiguous. As many voices proclaim him a hard core chauvinist as praise his feminist insights. Both camps are right because the play itself is self-consciously ambivalent about the gender relations on multiple levels: personal, representational, philosophical, ontological, political. The play both rejects the archetypal vision of feminine victimhood that Ophelia came to symbolize and at the same time, redefines it: "Ophelia" is both a Shakespearean heroine and a floating signifier that came to denote everything from beauty, pity, grief, melancholy, love, and longing to necromania, fear, and failure.[8] In "Ophelia," Müller creates an image of femininity that's victimized by its own impossibilities: she is a vision of radical feminism that cannot help but to eat its own tail. Since what Müller has created in *Hamletmachine* is not a character figure *per se*, but rather a poetic agglomeration of metaphors and images, his Ophelia, who is also Electra, Hamlet, and the Chorus, is multidimensional. On a political level, she represents revolutionary Rosa Luxemburg, the terrorist Ulrike Meinhoff, and the Charles Manson follower Susan Atkins; and on a personal level, as some have suggested, she stands for Müller's dead wife, Inge Schwenkner. Though there is no hard evidence, some critics have speculated that the domestic symbolism of *Hamletmachine* has personal implications for Müller, whose wife, Inge, committed suicide in 1966 (Kalb 1995: 226). Müller is on record as saying that, "The Ophelia-character is a criticism of Hamlet, consequently a self-critique; it contains autobiographical material dealing with the man–woman relationship of today" (quoted in Weber 1984: 51). Whatever the details of Müller's marriage, and Inge's suicide, whether he wanted it or not, from now on, Müller's sense of self, and his writing, would be mediated through the female corpse.[9] Inge's shadow persistently resurfaces in Müller writing, always frenzied and always on the rampage. Thus, in *Hamletmachine* too, Ophelia's battlefield is both "the ruins of Europe" and her home life, with everything it affords her. She "represents the 'return of the repressed' in multiple ways: on the political, historical, and psychological level male dominated society is confronted with the crimes upon which it is based and which come back to haunt it" (Rogowski 1993: 179). She starts the global uprising by trashing the place of her bondage masked as the place of comfort: "I smash the tools of my captivity, the chair the table the bed. I destroy the battlefield that was my home" (Müller 1984: 54). As Eva Brenner noted: "The private sphere of the home is exposed as the place of war and of sexual exploitation" (Brenner 1993: 77). Müller makes the private into the political and the political into the private.

Thus, *Hamletmachine* focuses on the motive of revenge that historically helped to awaken Germany's national sentiments and to define its masculine identity (which Müller himself is heir to), but this time, in this man/woman scenario, it is Ophelia who is the avenger. If in German cultural history it is Hamlet whose paternal obligation to revenge propelled the nationalization of the Hamlet myth, in *Hamletmachine*, it is Ophelia who adopts the masculine ethics of revenge and who is eventually undone by it. Contrasting her with Hamlet, Müller creates a kind of avenger of the feminist movement, one who as much fascinates as horrifies him. The Ophelia sequence begins in part two, entitled "Europe of Women." Kalb suggests that Müller, following Lenin, associated the European order based on family values with the paternal impulse, suggesting that any rebirth or overthrowing of the old order would have to begin with women (Kalb 1998a: 55). Ophelia's heart is a clock (a ticking time bomb?), and she begins by introducing her trope and her agenda:

> I am Ophelia. The one the river didn't keep. The woman dangling from the rope. The woman with her arteries cut open. The woman with the overdose. SNOW ON HER LIPS. The woman with the head in the gas oven. Yesterday I stopped killing myself. I am alone with my breasts my thighs my womb. I smash the tools of my captivity, the chair the table the bed. I destroy the battlefield that was my home. I fling open the doors so the wind gets in and the scream of the world. I smash the window. With my bleeding hands I tear the photos of the men I loved and who used me on the bed on the table on the chair on the floor. I set fire to my prison. I throw my clothes into the fire. I wrench the clock that was my heart from out of my breast. I go out on the street clothed in blood (Müller 1984: 54–55).

In his 1988 Weimar lecture on Shakespeare, Müller defined myth as "an aggregate, a machine on which an infinite number of others can be attached. It transports energy, until its acceleration bursts open the cultural sphere" (Müller 1995: 101). If Hamlet is a machine of patriarchal order, Ophelia/Electra is an exploding myth machine of the gender wars. Müller's Ophelia is, to borrow Nagele's phrase, "a phantom of a corpse," wrapped in the wet dress and the "fantastic garland" of male imagination. She is both the image of a Shakespearean heroine and an abstract, aesthetic figuration of a self-slaughtering female that "has usurped Western . . . consciousness" (Bloom 1998: 383) with an omnipotent image of "fair and unpolluted [female] flesh." She returns from the dead to "expressly *reject* the role required of her, as the lovelorn suicidal Shakespearean character, as lover or wife or woman to the dominant, violent male" (Teraoka 1985: 119). She rebels against the Ophelia trope and the necro-aesthetics and necro-ethics that structured the representation of a woman's beautified corpse as a site of female agency. "As opposed to auto-aggression and self-annihilation—characteristic of Shakespeare's

Ophelia—[Müller] proposes a radical break with the structure of
patriarchy if women are to regain identity" (Brenner 1994: 77). Ophelia,
who merely "stopped killing" herself, is already transgressing the taboo of
heterosexual fatality that structured the myth machine of her victimized
femininity. However, after the rebellious opening, Müller's play remains
ambiguous as to how truly liberated she can be. After the first diatribe in
part two, in part three, titled "Scherzo," Müller has Ophelia emerge from
the coffin. She "does a striptease," "blows HAMLET a kiss" and "steps
back into the coffin" (Müller 1984: 55). She enters the coffin willingly
naked and alive to make love to Claudius/HamletFather. As Kalb notices,
"clear-cut generalizations about the female rebellion are hard to make after
Ophelia willingly reenters a coffin, naked, with Claudius/HamletFather"
(Kalb 1998a: 56). How should Ophelia's reentering the coffin be
interpreted? Does she "stop killing" herself because she is already dead, or
was she never really "revived" in the first place? Or is her aggression
against herself wrapped in the symbolic language that she cannot escape?

In his essay on "Femininity," Freud writes: "The suppression of
women's aggressiveness which is prescribed for them constitutionally and
imposed on them socially favours the development of powerful
masochistic impulses. .... Thus masochism, as people say, is truly
feminine" (Freud 1961: 116). Freud's text implies that the female
masochism is socially and politically motivated. Rejecting both the
conditions "imposed on her socially" and the role of masochist that Freud
ascribed to her feminine nature, Müller's Ophelia appears to channel her
supposed masochistic impulse into sadistic violence against the other. In
her first segment, she "sets fire to her prison" and "goes out on the street
clothed in blood," ready to inflict as much pain as she once received. Her
sadism is "a culmination" of her oppression, as though the sufferings she
has undergone "allowed the exercise of evil they once prohibited"
(Deleuze 1991: 39). No longer directing her aggression against herself, she
directs it "outward against the real oppressor, patriarchal society" (Brenner
1993: 77). She is a victim, but "a victim with a vengeance, clear-sighted
and highly unsentimental" (Fischlim 2000: 209–210). From a masochist
she turns into a sadist on a mission. But why, then, in the next scene does
Müller have her re-enter the coffin? Does she confirm or displace the
masochistic ethos? Is she turning the violence yet again against herself, or
is she merely displacing the masochistic self and its preconditions?

5. Femininity and the Ethos of Revenge

Historically, Shakespearean Ophelia represented the other, self-destructive, feminine Germany. Müller's Ophelia represents this historical paradox: even though man's masculine self-identity is defined by his willingness to revenge (to die and to kill in the name of his patriarch), a woman who adopts such ethics does not become a man, yet she ceases to be a "woman." Müller associates his "Ophelia" with actual historical figures: she exhibits characteristics of the Marxist revolutionary Rosa Luxemburg, killed in 1919, but also the anarchist/murderer Susan Atkins, a.k.a. Sadie, of the Manson group, who helped to perpetrate some of the gang's bloodiest murders, and the leftist urban guerilla terrorist Ulrike Meinhoff of the "Baader-Meinhoff Gang" of the 1960s (Teraoka 1985: 111). But she also has some traits of the 70s radical Valerie Solanas, best known for shooting Andy Warhol in 1968.[10] A few critics have pointed out that among other things, Müller's Ophelia, like Solanas, represents the military aspect of the 1970s feminist movement. In this spirit, J. M. Dudley suggests that, "Within this Other, feminine space of representation, Ophelia's existence is defined (in opposition to both Hamlet's and Gertrude's) by her position as a radical feminist" (Dudley 1992: 567). Constructing his Ophelia from the bits and pieces of female mass murderer, revolutionary, cult follower, and military feminist, Müller aims to emphasize the cruelty that a female is capable of, while at the same time questioning the ethical position of a violent female subject.

The poster child for militant feminism, Solanas advocated radical misandry. In 1968, she fired three shots into Andy Warhol, seeing him as the quintessential image of "male leech." Regarded by some as a martyr upon her release from prison in 1971, though eventually dying alone and destitute in a welfare hotel in San Francisco in 1988, Solanas has been hailed as "the first outstanding champion of women's rights" and "one of the most important spokeswomen of the feminist movement" (Ronell 2004a: 30). Norman Mailer called her "Robespierre of feminism" (Ronell 2004b: 10). In 1977, the same year when Muller reportedly wrote *Hamletmachine*, Solanas self-published her *SCUM Manifesto*. In 1977, two interviews with her appeared in the *Village Voice* (in July and August).[11] By then, Solanas's story, partially on account of Warhol, was widely known in both the U.S. and abroad. In 1975, Müller visited the U.S. for the first time (he was a writer-in-residence at the University of Texas in Austin and then he travelled extensively throughout the country). It is highly unlikely that he hadn't heard of her.

Indeed, the similarities between *Hamletmachine* and *SCUM Manifesto* are uncanny. For one, there is structural resemblance: the manifesto-like format of Ophelia's diatribes, her anger, and her violent misandry parallels Solanas' rant. For another, Müller was fascinated by and somewhat identified with Warhol. In fact, *HamletMachine* (H.M.—Heiner Müller) is purportedly also titled after Warhol's famous quote: "I want to be a machine … The reason I'm painting this way is that I want to be a machine and I feel that whatever I do and do machine-like is what I want to do." (Originally quoted in Swenson, G.R. (1963 November). "What is Pop Art?" *Art News*. 62. p. 26.) Müller's translation of Shakespeare's collective works, published under the title *Shakespeare Factory,* is also a bow to Warhol, whose industrial art studio, where he mechanically reproduced ready-made images, was widely known as the "Factory." The most striking distinction between males and females sketched out by Solanas in her manifesto is precisely the comparison of males to machines.[12] "To call a man an animal is to flatter him;" she wrote, "he's a machine" (Solanas 2004: 37). Warhol was, for Solanas an archetypical machine-man, which seemed accurate in light of how others also described him: "Warhol was irremediably cold – frozen, a black hole of nothingness in which everything disappeared" (Kuspit 1998: 85). Müller himself called him "a car-body without a motor" (Kalb 1998: 223). Was *Hamletmachine* modeled on Solanas and Warhol's relationship, with Warhol as an unraveling Hamlet/MACHINE and Solanas as an avenging feminist Ophelia who shot him?

The other common thread which appears in both *SCUM* and *Hamletmachine* is a suggestion that women's liberation is foremost a rejection of reproductive function, and thus, it inevitably leads to the cessation of the human species, something about which both Müller and Solanas are ambivalent. In the final scene of *Hamletmachine*, Ophelia recites a violent diatribe against motherhood and its trappings:

> This is Electra speaking. In the heart of darkness. Under the sun of torture. To the captials of the world. In the name of the victims. I eject all the sperm I have received. I turn the milk of my breasts into lethal poison. I take back the world I gave birth to. I choke between my thighs the world I gave birth to. I bury it in my womb. Down the happiness of submission. Long live hate and contempt, rebellion and death. When she walks through your bedrooms carrying butcher knives you'll know the truth (Müller 1984: 58).

By taking back "the world she gave birth to," Ophelia both reclaims the position of woman as mother, without whom the world/the man would not exist, "reclaiming her womanly capacity to propagate the world" as Richard Halpern put it (Halpern 1997: 275–76), and at the same time she rejects it. Her role and power is to reproduce the world over and over again, like a machine, and for once she refuses to do so. Müller suggests that the female is enslaved by the mechanical reproduction of the human species: motherhood—like sex—is a source of exploitation. In contrast, Müller's Ophelia embraces the ethics of "hate, contempt, rebellion and death." She "chokes the world," "bur[ies] it in her womb" and, like Lady Macbeth, turns her milk into poison. This is an ethics of death that has no future. Raddatz points out that "the emancipation of women in Müller's later plays does not foresee a fair participation of women in society's development . . . and it does not form a breaking point within occidental history, it rather falls in one with its definitive endpoints" (qtd. in Brenner 1994: 79). In her manifesto, Solanas makes a similar point: "Should a certain percentage of women be set aside by force to serve as brood mares for the species? Obviously this will not do. ... Why should there be future generations? What is their purpose?" (Solanas: 68). Like for Müller, for Solanas too, the apocalyptic end of the world is a side effect of women's liberation.

6. Who Is Afraid of Sadean Woman?

Focusing on the ethos of murder and revenge, Müller follows Artaud's call to "stage ...a Tale by the Marquis de Sade" (Artaud: 99), fashioning his Ophelia on the Sadean heroine. In Sade, there are only two kinds of women: the virtuous victim and the libertine villainess, for whom murder, theft, and prostitution are everyday activities. If Sade's victims are incapable of rebelling, incapable of raising their hands against their oppressor, even when given such a chance and even in self-defense, Sade's female villain unflinchingly wreaks havoc, death, and destruction . Carter comments:

> Sade's heroines, those who become libertines, accept damnation, by which I mean this exile from human life, as a necessary fact of life. This is the nature of the libertine. They model themselves upon libertine men. . . . So Sade creates a museum of woman-monsters. He cuts up the bodies of women and reassembles them in the shapes of his own delirium. He renews all the ancient wounds, every one, and makes them bleed again as if they will never stop bleeding (Carter: 25–26).

Modeling herself on the libertine man, the Sadean woman steps outside of the limits of representation, beyond good and evil, beyond ethics, and into the monstrous. But, as Simone de Beauvoir suggests, the cruelty of the Sadean female is a direct result of her fundamental *status quo* as a victim. Beauvoir deconstructs the irony of this dialectic:

> [I]t is through a mythical dialectic that [Sade] gives them [women] the most triumphant roles in his novels. Their wickedness makes a striking contrast with the traditional gentleness of their sex. When they overcome their natural abjection by committing crime, they demonstrate much more brilliantly than any man that no situation can dampen the ardor of a bold spirit. But if, in imagination, they become first-rate martinets, it is because they are, in reality, born victims. (Beauvoir: 25)

Sade's villainesses become sadists because they are born to be masochists. They only exercise their cruelty with furious delight to avenge themselves for the sufferings they have undergone. It is the ethics which Müller's adopts for his Ophelia. The last lines of the play ("When she walks through your bedrooms carrying butcher knives you'll know the truth") suggest a violent rupture of both the text and the gender relations. As Blau framed it: "The immediate truth of the butcher knives is what is tearing the text apart" (Blau: 69). Müller constructs an idea of femininity in terms of a masculine ethics, thus the image he creates crosses the lines of gender and its representation: Ophelia is a cipher of images and literary allusions. She is femininity detached from itself and from any essential embodiment. As such she symbolizes the "closure of representation" and, by extension, the end of the world as we know it. Like the Sadean woman, Ophelia/Electra not only rejects femininity and the machinery of reproduction it entails, she embraces the Sadean ethics of death, thus embracing the possibility of the end of the world.[13] Müller suggests that she (or whatever "she" means in this context) will not stop until she destroys the world that oppressed her, through both direct violence against it (taking it to the street), and indirect refusal to be trapped by her biological function. Halpern comments on the final scene: "Ophelia smashes the machinery of her repression, thereby freeing herself from indefinite repetition of her role. Yet her triumph does not ring in utopia. Instead, it ends the world ... Adopting the politics of the death drive, Ophelia rejects Hamlet's model of dilapidated repetition, opting instead for one immense revolution in which everything is reabsorbed into its maternal source and smothered there, in a kind of implosive sequel to the original Big Bang" (Halpern: 275–76). Rejecting the death-ethics and death-aesthetic inscribed within the definition of the feminine self (the suicidal impulse, fetishized in the image of her corpse, that leads the female to be "shattered by something intrinsic to [her] own being") (Hegel

1975: 1217), Müller's Ophelia at the same time appears to embrace an alternative death-ethic: one based on her refusal of the other. In other words, adopting *literally* the male-created ethos of death and violence, she threatens the world as a whole.

7. From Coffin to Straitjacket: the Return of the Same

Fundamentally, Müller's Ophelia begins as an iconic victim and ends as an iconic victim. Not only does she willingly re-enter the coffin, but in the final scene, while she is pronouncing her last lines, Ophelia/Electra is strapped to the wheelchair, and mummified by two men dressed in "white smocks" (psychiatrists?), who wrap her up in white gauze (a straitjacket?) "from bottom to top" (Müller 1984: 58). Weber comments on this final tableau: "The final scene with Ophelia being wrapped in white bandages and finally being silenced after having cursed and rejected the world as we know it, is probably the most devastating verdict of contemporary society ever written for the stage" (Weber 1980: 140). In one German production, this last image evoked such strong emotions in the viewing audience that some audience members rushed to the actress's help, and proceeded to unwrap her. While trying to alter, inflect, attenuate and displace the Ophelia myth machine, Müller's Ophelia in the wheelchair is a literalization of the clinical aspect of the Ophelia syndrome. But it also represents a peculiar paradox of the feminist discourse: a closure of gender as representation.

In the clinical discourse of Nineteenth-Century Europe, the Shakespearean Ophelia came to represent a peculiar female malady of death: a psychological predisposition, based on one's femininity, to madness and suicide. In other words, femininity was a medical condition that would inevitably require medical attention. In 1833, George Farren considered Shakespeare's description of mad Ophelia an ideal example of a clinical case of female insanity. He wrote: "It is impossible to conceive of any thing more perfect than the picture of disease given by Shakespeare in this scene of Ophelia's. Every medical professor who is familiar with cases of insanity will freely acknowledge its truth" (Farren: 59). For Farren, Shakespeare's description of Ophelia's insanity has a clinical quality. Elaine Showalter suggests that, "illustrations of Ophelia, notably a series of pictures produced by Delacroix between 1830 and 1850, inspired by Harriet Smithson's portrayal, played a major role in the theoretical construction of female insanity." Showalter continues: "Ophelia became the prototype not only of the deranged woman in Victorian literature and art but also of the young female asylum patient" (Showalter 1985: 80, 90).

Soon, doctors began to diagnose some of their female mental patients with "Ophelia." Conolly in his 1863 *Study of Hamlet* wrote:

> Never did a poet's pen draw so touching and so true a portrait of madness fallen on a delicate and affectionate girl. . . . Our asylum for ruined minds now and then presents remarkable illustrations of the fatal malady, so that even casual visitors recognize in the wards an Ophelia; the same young years, the same faded beauty, the same fantastic dress and interrupted song. (Conolly: 177–78).

Actresses of that time, such as Ellen Tracy or Harriet Smithson, visited mental hospitals in order to study young mentally disturbed girls to prepare for their roles of Ophelia.[14] The most dramatic insertion of Ophelia into the clinical discourse was a series of photographs taken by Dr. Hugh Welsh Diamond (1809–1886), who was a superintendent of female patients at the Surrey County Lunatic Asylum in Springfield and a member of the Photographic Society of London. Beginning in 1851, Dr. Diamond took a series of photographs of young women to illustrate various cases of female insanity. One photo of an "Ophelia" is especially disturbing. To prepare a girl for the photograph, Dr. Diamond wrapped her up in a black veil (it was the theatrical tradition at the time to have Ophelia wear a black veil during her mad scene as a sign of mourning for Polonius), and put garlands of flowers in her hair.[15] For Dr. Diamond, Ophelia was an ideal madwoman. Stylizing his patient to look like Shakespeare's heroine, he was able to create a discourse, if only a literary one, around her insanity. Shakespeare's story provided the cause of madness, and helped Dr. Diamond to write a psychiatric diagnosis and the story behind it (abandoned, traumatized, deflowered, and so forth). Representing Ophelia as a typical madwoman, who also exhibited typical feminine characteristics (such as sensitivity, obedience, innocence, fragility, and so forth), also contributed to the Nineteenth-Century construction of femininity as unstable and self-destructive. The practice of diagnosing girls with Ophelia syndrome was widespread, and also influenced Jean-Martin Charcot (1825–1893) and his psychiatric research on female insanity. Lehman points out that "Dr. Diamond's manipulation of the madwomen under his care, and his attempts to make them conform to his ideal of madness, foreshadow Charcot's work at the end of the century. Charcot's patients were also coached for the cameras, and sometimes instructed to perform Shakespearian heroines while under hypnosis" (Lehman: 53–54). Freud was a student at Charcot's clinic for four months in 1885 and 1886, and considered Charcot his greatest professional inspiration. To what degree were Freud's own theories on femininity, female hysteria, and female masochism modeled on the image of Ophelia?

Wrapping Ophelia in a white gauze in the final scene,[16] Müller is returning to the pre-established European tradition of representing her figure as mentally instable and in need of medical attention. This last tableau plays on a Becketian, by now somewhat clichéd, image of a wheelchair as an existential metaphor for emotional confinement, to literalize both the clinical and the political aspect of the Ophelia malady. The image suggests that a) her rebellion is silenced, whether by external force or the inner turmoil of its own paradoxes and impossibilities, and b) she was never sane in the first place, her raging diatribes as insane as Shakespeare's Ophelia's mad songs. Müller commented on this final authorial decision:

> The final scene is defined by this feeling: that it is not too late; the feeling that the revolution can now only exist in a submarine traveling around the globe. Then, in writing it, I changed this again, so that the revolution, as represented by Ophelia/Electra, is finally silenced, even in the submarine, by the psychiatrists or whatever we assume these men in their white smocks are. (qtd. in Weber 1980: 140)

In a 1990 Berlin production of the play that Müller directed, he goes even further, having Ophelia "consumed by a large flame" (Hortmann: 433). In the context of German nationalism, if Hamlet revenging is Germany and Ophelia a kind of failed alternative to the ethos of revenge, what, then, does her symbolic mummification mean in the larger political framework?

Some Shakespearean critics interpret Ophelia's madness as a strategy, similar to Hamlet's, to give herself a space of freedom in which to say whatever she wants: to give voice to her helpless rage: "Her insanity incorporates a clarity that we do not usually attribute to madness" (Coursen 2001: 59). Others suggest that Ophelia comes to terms with herself through her madness.[17] Felman suggests that any representation of a madwoman should be viewed as "both as *mad* and as *not mad*" (Felman: 18). Standing outside of ethics, a madwoman cannot be judged as ethically and legally responsible.[18] Within the context of such interpretation of the Shakespearean story, Müller's Ophelia, who avenges herself, is more a continuation of Shakespeare's character than it might seem at first glance: she illuminates the darker political undertone of the story. Within the context of Germany's historically gendered national self-definition, she represents an impasse of that discourse: the myth of masculinity turns into thin air once she tries to adopt it. Moreover, confining his Ophelia to a straitjacket, Müller places her outside the realm of the rational, at least on the symbolic level, thus questioning the ethical status of a female avenger, the purpose and the outcome of her revenge.

The stage directions for the last scene read that Ophelia is in a "deep sea," with "fish, debris, dead bodies and limbs drifting by" (Müller 1984: 58). Thus, Müller not only returns her to the phallocentric trope of femininity as a disease that needs to be contained, but also to the "watery grave" from which he resurrected her in the first scene. Such a symbolic return to the point of departure also signifies the circularity and paralysis of the feminist discourse (the trope of a victim turns one into a victim; there is no escape from victimhood), as well as the intrinsic paradox of the ethics of cruelty she adopts. Since it is a male ethics, in adopting it, the course of Ophelia's feminine self eventually comes to a halt, becomes paralyzed. Her radicalism is both liberating and incapacitating. After they have finished wrapping her up, the two men in white smocks exit, leaving Ophelia on stage, "motionless in her white wrappings" (Müller 1984: 58). She is done for, finished, undone. What kind of undoing does this immobility signify? Adopting an ethics of cruelty, Müller defines her, like Medea, in terms of "an honour code traditionally restricted to the male warrior. It is this male value system [based on violence and revenge] which she has accepted for herself . . . " (Rogowski: 174). Her rebellion, brutal and bloody, is a mirror reflection of the violence she (or rather her figuration) has received at the hands of Western culture. But on the other hand, because she internalizes the male value system, Müller seems to suggest, it "ultimately destroys her [feminine] identity" (Rogowski: 174). Walsh describes the idea:

> Müller produces a chilling finale in which the language of subversion and active resistance is coded as pathologized violence, in effect providing the play's moral. Ophelia's comments, all directed on some level as a strike against hegemonic inscription, signal her as not merely unruly but monstrous. Her abnegation of motherhood, nurture, and other cultural expectations of femininity mark her as the Lady Macbeth-like "unsexed" woman, whose ambition and lust for power borders on the demonic, while her identification with Electra positions her as relentless, single-minded, and willful in seeking a vengeance that is outside prescribed social codes. (Walsh: 31)

Walsh falls prey to a known patriarchal sentiment: he cannot conceive of the idea of a female who would reject her gendered victim status but simultaneously retain the status of an ethical subject. Rejection of "cultural expectations of femininity," and "ambition and lust for power" equals monstrosity. Apparently, a female should not have ambition and/or "lust for power" if she is to retain her human quality. "Violence, the convulsive form of the active, male principle, is a matter for men, whose sex gives them the right to inflict pain as a sign of mastery" (Carter: 22). Whereas male gender identity rests on the universal principle of the phallic experience, which includes "ambition," "lust for power," and "pathologized violence" within its system of symbolic codes, "unsexed" woman becomes nothing, the "demonic" Other. When she is not woman, not a mother, not a lover, not a victim, she is nothing. Rejecting her reproductive and nurturing potential, Ophelia/Electra sheds the feminine ethos, but because she simultaneously sheds the female "self," she comes to stand as if *outside* of the universal law of the patriarchal exchange, "outside prescribed social codes." Instead of achieving the status of ethical subject, she comes to stand as if *outside* of ethics. Her image explodes into the violent figuration of a woman who goes "beyond the limit of human" and becomes, in Walsh's words, "monstrous." Müller's Ophelia represents the impasse and limits of the feminist ethics framed by the masculine code of revenge. Müller, it seems, like Walsh, cannot conceive of her becoming the cruel other: the cruelty that she wants to inflict incapacitates her. As Brenner suggests: "Müller offers a dialectic: the force of her hate is so strong that it might be questionable if it will not destroy herself" (Brenner: 81). Müller suggests that there seem to be only two ways of dealing with patriarchal oppression: either acceptance or terrorism, and both ultimately fail her. She symbolizes the impasse of the impasse, the impossible of the impossible, and the paradox of her gender. Submerging her in the sea, and strapping her to the wheelchair, is Müller also suggesting that her revenge, like Hamlet's/Germany's, is destined to failure?

8. The Ends of a Woman

Kalb suggests that *both* Hamlet and Ophelia are "victims of a common identity crisis and allies in a common project to dismantle the representational frame of that crisis." He continues:

> Gestures like Ophelia's tearing of "the photographs of the men whom I loved" and the similar "tearing of the photograph of the author" in section four suggest that iconography, representation itself, is under attack as much as any male–author-principle. (Kalb 1998a: 56)

According to Kalb, Muller deconstructs the representation itself, the man as representation, and this "crisis of representation," as Derrida would say, has fundamentally humanistic foundation: man means here a humanity at large, not a phallic subject. This implies that "the end of man" also encompasses the end of woman. However, because within the phallocentric discourse, the definition of a 'man' is definition of a man (as a male), "the end of man" does not encompass the end of woman. Femininity both belongs and does not belong to humanity as such. Woman is and she is not a human being. In *Gender Trouble*, Butler writes:

> [Irigaray argues that] woman constitute a paradox, if not a contradiction, within the discourse of identity itself. Women are the 'sex' which is not 'one.' Within a language pervasively masculinist, a phallocentric language, women constitute the unrepresentable. In other words, women represent the sex that cannot be thought, a linguistic absence and opacity (Butler: 14).

If male sexuality and male subjectity is taken as a point of departure in the power structure of linguistic relations, female sexuality and female subjectivity will always/already be a reflection of male sexuality and male subjectivity. As Butler points out "The female sex is thus also the subject that is not one. The relation between masculine and feminine cannot be represented in a signifying economy in which the masculine constitutes the closed circle of signifier and signified" (Butler: 15). Female always/already will be a sign that is not one. Never faced with the question of whether she should be or not be—because she already will be and not be at the same time—she will never also have to answer it, either to herself or to the other. As a subject that is not one, woman, therefore, is also an ethical agent that is not one. In relationship to a man, she is not an ethical subject, and she has no ethical responsibility toward the male as a fellow human being. As close circuit of significations, the phallocentric dialectic precludes the universalization of its human condition. The femininity is outside of patriarchy's linguistic, ethical, philosophical, as well as social, economic, legal and political discourse. It exists only within its own parameters of gender, negotiated by the reproductive needs of the species. Thus, femininity is not representable. But if woman as such does not exist, how can one stage/enact the end of a woman if she is always/already not? If the feminine exists only as representation, would the end of representation mean the end of femininity or rather, would it mean its beginning? Writing about Solana's manifesto, Ronell points out that it was written a year before Derrida's essay on the end of the man (Solanas wrote her manifesto in 1967 and Derrida wrote his essay in 1968). Writing his essay, Derrida was "concerned with the excess of man, which Solanas, we could say, enacted. Where he exposed the Greek ideal of anthropos, she went for the jugular of referential man, busting through layers of philosophical history to put out her own 'ends of man,' her own limit case of the classical unity of man" (Solanas: 2). In other words, Solanas takes Derrida's call for 'the end of man' literally. What end of man/woman is Müller staging? By making Ophelia into a violent avenger, is he releasing her from her ethical responsibility, or is he suggesting that she is fundamentally trapped in the ethical paradox of her gender: not an ethical subject in the first place, she can never perform an act of revenge; she is beyond judgment, beyond responsibility, and beyond rights. She is, however, within the limits of brute force. Is her final paralysis then a closure of representation? A closure of gender? A closure of ethics? Or the limits of the male discourse? The end of representation? The end of the world? Writing about Solanas in *The Nation* in 2004, Dederer again compared her life to Sylvia Plath's, asking:

> What if Sylvia Plath had shot Ted Hughes instead of gassing herself? How would we read her work? Would we still dream of her as a beautiful woman? .... Plath's suicide and Solanas's attempted murder of Warhol might be considered the two major acts of feminist violence of the 1960s (Dedere: 55).

If Plath's self-aimed violence is framed, as Dederer suggests, within the phallocentric discourse of self-killing female as "the most poetical topic in the world," Solanas' violence aimed at the other is the most troubling topic in the world. Indeed, what would happen if instead of trying to kill herself, Elizabeth Hauptmann had tried to kill Brecht? What would happen if instead of becoming insane, Vivienne Haigh-Wood would have driven Elliot insane? And finally, what would happen if Inge Schwenkner killed Müller instead of killing herself? Would there be *Opheliamachine* instead of *Hamletmachine*? What would Ophelia say then?

Notes

[1] See also Mosse, G. (1996). *The Image of Man: The Creation of Modern Masculinity*. New York: Oxford University Press.

[2] In 1835, Heine was the first one who ominously noted that in the eyes of German youth, the image of Hamlet has a Messianic aspect: "The German youth love Hamlet, because they feel that 'time is out of joint.' They also yearn for that which they are called to restore." (Quoted in Pfister, M. (1986). "Germany is Hamlet: The History of a Political Interpretation." *New Comparison: A Journal of Comparative and General Literary Studies* 2:115.)

[3] The idea of Shakespeare foreshadowing the German national character in *Hamlet* can be found earliest in Heinrich Theodor Rötscher in *Die Kunst der dramatischen Darstellung zweiter Teil* (Berlin, 1844): 127f.

[4] See Pfister, M. (1986). "Germany is Hamlet: The History of a Political Interpretation." *New Comparison: A Journal of Comparative and General Literary Studies* 2: 106–126.

[5] Ibid.

[6] See Minogue, V. (1989) "Rimbaud's Ophelia." *French Studies* 43: 423–436.

[7] See Nagele, R. (2002 December). "Phantom of a Corpse: Ophelia from Rimbaud to Brecht." *MLN, 117*(5): 1069–1082; Wüerffel Bodo, S. (1985). *Ophelia: Figure and Alienation.* Berne: Francke; Stuby, A. M. (1992). *Liebe, Tod und Wasserfrau. Mythen des Weiblichen in der Literatur.* Wiesbaden: 163–216; and Flower, B. (1954). "The Drowned Girl. Rimbaud's 'Ophélie' and the German Literature." *GRM* 4: 108–119.

[8] Wilson for example, "split" the roles of both Ophelia and Hamlet onto multiple actors. Writing about the 1986 Wilson production of Müller's *Hamletmachine*, Rogoff pointed out that "oddly, the work could be more accurately entitled OPHELIAMACHINE in this version, Wilson giving a more emotionally charged emphasis to the women than he does to the men. . . . in this respect, it may be that Wilson merely offered a more clearly defined Müller, one who can't help seeing women as victims frightening him to death" (Rogoff: 57). Indeed, Rogoff is right on target, as Müller said that he imagined an American version of the play staged with Ophelia as the main character (Weber 1984: 51). Wilson, with whom Müller closely collaborated between 1984 and 1988, staged *Hamletmachine* with students of the Tisch School of the Arts, New York University. In Wilson's version, the many copies of Ophelia, frozen in slow time/motion, create a psychosomatic aura of entrapment. Reciting their lines in monotones, they loom on stage like Macbeth's witches. In some scenes, forming two rows, Ophelias surround Hamlet and his double, like a jury giving a verdict. In Kafkaesque fashion, they look almost robotic, and there is something almost fascist in their severity. Finally, the Hamlets fall to the ground, and the Ophelias hover over them like famished harpies. In yet another scene, one Ophelia marches like a soldier, while others chant maddeningly. As Rogoff poignantly noticed, with his production Wilson managed to capture the frightening and disjointed quality of Müller's Ophelia.

[9] Müller and Inge met in 1954-55 while he was working for the League of German Writers. At that time she was already an award-winning playwright (she won the Erich Weinert Medal for *The Women's Brigade*) Together, Müller and Schwenkner wrote *The Scab* (1958), Müller's "best known and most-staged production play," awarded the prestigious Heinrich Mann's Prize, and *The Correction* (performed, 1958; published 1959). In his first English language anthology of Muller's plays, translated under his guidelines, Carl Weber never mentions Inge's authorship role in *The Correction*. In fact, in his introduction to the anthology, Weber does not even mention her once, as if she never existed.

[10] She appeared in his 1967 film, *I, a Man*, and was his receptionist for a few months. Warhol tolerated her and even promised to produce her play. However, he lost her manuscript; she thought he kept it to steal it. Emotionally disturbed, paranoid, and feeling used, Solanas shot him when he failed to keep his promise. (For a dramatization of the events, see M. Harron's 1996 film *I Shot Andy Warhol*, or C. Kreitzer's play *Valerie Shoots Andy*.)

¹¹ See Howard Smith. "Valerie Solanas Interview." *Village Voice*. July 25, 1977: 32.; and "Valerie Solanas Replies." *Village Voice*. August 1, 1977: 28. *Village Voice* also published an interview with her in 1968. See Robert Marmortein. "SCUM Goddess: A Winter Memory of Valerie Solanas." *Village Voice*. June 13, 1968: 9, 10, 20.

¹² Avital Ronell suggests that Solanas's manifesto was a direct response to the violent misogyny and the cult of the machine of Marinetti's 1909 "Futurist Manifesto." In his manifesto glorifying war, militarism and the coming age of the machine, Marinnetti also propagates "scorn for woman." He writes: "We will glorify war .... Beautiful ideas worth dying for, and scorn for woman. ... we will destroy .... feminism." ("The Founding Manifesto of Futurism," *Le Figaro*, Paris: February 20, 1909.) Though Ronell is right to point out the counter-discoursive quality of Solanas' work (relative to Marinetti's), what is even more interesting to point out is the difference in the reception of both manifestos. Whereas Marinetti's misogyny was acceptable and printed right away in the mainstream Parisian newspaper, Solanas' equally pathological misandry (even though it was written sixty years later) was viewed as psychopathology. This shows how normalized misogyny is (was), and how abnormal appears (appeared) equally violent androphobia.

¹³ Sade's violent eschatology is anti-humanistic and a-theological. His libertine dreams of the end of the symbolic universe, "the absolute death—the destruction, the eradication, of the [natural cycle of generation and corruption], which then liberates nature from its own laws and opens the way for the creation of new forms of life *ex nihilo*" (Zizek 1989: 34).

¹⁴ Medical interpretations of Shakespeare were very popular at that time. Dr. John Charles Bucknill wrote two books on the subject: *The Medical Knowledge of Shakespeare* (London: Longman, 1860), and *The Mad Folk of Shakespeare; Psychological Essays* (London and Cambridge: Macmillan, 1867). Another example is John Moyes' 1886 doctoral thesis, *Medicine and Kindred Arts in the Plays of Shakespeare*. It was first published in 1896, and the appended bibliography of "Shakespearean Medicine" included forty-six Nineteenth-Century medical and psychiatric interpretation of Shakespeare. The practice of providing medical interpretation for Shakespearean characters was so popular, in fact, that at some point it was difficult to say whether the characters were merely diagnosed with already recognizable diseases, or whether they provided models for new mental and physiological ailments. For further reading on the subject, see Bynum, W. F. & Neve, M. (1985). "Hamlet on the Couch." In Bynum, W. F., R.Porter, and M. Shepherds (Eds.), *The Anatomy of Madness: Essays in the History of Psychiatry, 2*: 289–304. London: Tavistock.

¹⁵ For the story of Dr. Diamond, see Nicoletti, L. (1999). "Resuscitating Ophelia: Images of suicide and suicidal insanity in nineteenth-century England." (Doctoral Dissertation, University of Wisconsin).

¹⁶ In the same spirit, in some recent film adaptations and stage productions of *Hamlet*, the director chooses to emphasize the madness and confinement of Ophelia by having her wrapped up in a strait jacket. For example, in Kenneth Branagh's 1996 film, she is bound and given water treatments. For a brief history

of various interpretations of Shakespeare's Ophelia in modern *Hamlet* productions, see Coursen, H.R. (2001). *Ophelia in Performance in the Twentieth century*. In C. Kiefer (Ed). *The Myth and Madness of Ophelia*: 53–61. Amherst: Mead Art Museum.

[17] See Philip, R. (1991). "The Shattered Glass: The Story of (O)phelia." *Hamlet Studies* 13.1–2: 73–84.

[18] Foucault suggests that historically madmen, and criminals about to be executed, had a certain space of political freedom in which they could say anything they wanted. In *Discipline and Punishment* (1995), Foucault writes about eighteenth-century executions:

> If the crowd gathered round the scaffold, it was not simply to witness the sufferings of the condemned man or to excite the anger of the executioner: it was also to hear an individual who had nothing more to lose curse the judges, the laws, the government and religion. The public execution allowed the luxury of these momentary saturnalia, when nothing remained to prohibit or to punish. Under the protection of imminent death, the criminal could say everything and the crowd cheered. (Foucault 1995: 60)

In the same manner, the mad were seen as a source of truth. In *Madness and Civilization* (1988), Foucault writes:

> [T]he truth comes to light, in and through madness, which, provoked by the illusion of denouement, actually resolves the real imbroglio of which it is both cause and effect. . . . Madness is the false punishment of false solution, but by its own virtue it brings to light the real problem, which can then be truly resolved. It conceals beneath error the secret enterprise of truth." (Foucault 1988: 33)

Death and madness allowed for the moment of truth; it represented a purging of social consciousness. Standing outside of the ethical order, criminals about to be executed, as well as the insane, were given leeway to point out all disparities within the social and political structures. Thus, to escape into madness also meant to escape outside of the constraints of one's social position and social relations, into the "secret enterprise of truth." To be outside of reason meant to operate within the freedom of logic that unraveled the limits of reason. Representing the mad as truth bearers was also part of theatrical convention, as Guilfoyle (1980) notes: "characters who go mad in renaissance drama frequently speak more truth, and deeper truth than when sane, and this can be said of Ophelia" (Guilfoyle: 6).

Work Cited

Artaud, A. (1958). *The Theater and Its Double*. New York: Grove Press.

Barnett, D. (1980). *Literature vs. Theater: Textual problems and theatrical realization in the later plays of Heiner Müller*. Berne: Peter Lang Publishing.

Beauvoir, S, de. (1966). "Must We Burn Sade?" *The 120 Days of Sodom and Other Writings*. Trans. Annette Michelson. New York: Grove Press.

Berkowitz, G. M. (1986). "Shakespeare at the Edinburgh Festival." *Shakespeare Quarterly, 37* (2): 227–229.

Blau, H. (1987). "The Audition of Dream and Events." *Drama Review. 31* (3): 59–73.

Bloom, H. (1998). *Shakespeare: the Invention of the Human.* New York: Riverhead Books.

Brenner, E. (1994). "HAMLETMACHINE Onstage: a Critical Analysis of Heiner Müller's Play in Production." DAI. New York University.

—. (1992). "Heiner Müller Directs Heiner Müller." *The Drama Review, 36* (1): 160–168.

Butler, J. (1999). *Gender Trouble: Feminism and the Subversion of Identity* New York: Routledge.

Bynum, W. F. & Neve, M. (1985). "Hamlet on the Couch." *The Anatomy of Madness: Essays in the History of Psychiatry, 2.* Ed. Bynum, W.F., Roy Porter, and Michael Shepherds. London: Tavistock: 289-304.

Caravjal, C. (1989). *"Die Hamletmaschine* on Two Stages: Heiner Müller's Allegories and the Problem of Translation." *Text and Presentation, Vol. 9.* Ed. K. V. Hartigan. Vol. 9. Lanham: University Press of America: 39–49.

Carter, A. (1978). *The Sadeian Woman and the Ideology of Pornography.* New York: Pantheon Books.

Case, S. E. (1981). "Developments in Post-Brechtian Political Theater: The Plays of Heiner Müller." DAI. University of California, Berkeley.

—. (1983). "From Bertolt Brecht to Heiner Müller.*" Performing Arts Journal* 19: 94–102.

Chambers, R. (1971). "L'Ange et l'automate: Variations sure le mythe de l'actrice de Nerval a Proust. Paris: Archives de Lettres Modernes." Quoted in Lehman, Amy (1996). "Theatricality, Madness and Mesmerism: Nineteenth-century Female Performers." DAI. University of Indiana: 11.

Cohen, M. (1989). *'Hamlet': In My Mind's Eye.* Athens: University of Georgia Press.

—. (1996). *Fashioning Masculinity: National Identity and Language in the Eighteenth Century.* New York: Routledge.

Cohn, A. (1865). *Shakespeare in Germany in the Sixteenth and Seventeenth Centuries: An Account of English Actors in Germany and the Netherlands and of the Plays Performed by Them During the Same Period.* London: Asher.

Conolly, J. (1863). *A Study of Hamlet.* London: Edward Moxon.

Coursen. H. R. (2001). "Ophelia in Performance in the Twentieth Century." *The Myth and Madness of Ophelia.* Ed., C. Kiefer. Amherst: Mead Art Museum: 53-61.

Dederer, C. (2004 June 14). "Cutting Remarks." *The Nation*: 55.

Deem, M. (1996). "From Bobbitt to SCUM: Re-memberment, Scatological Rhetorics, and Feminist Strategies in the Contemporary United States." *Public Culture*: 3, 8.

Deleuze, G. (1991). *Masochism: Coldness and Cruelty.* New York: Zone Books.

Derrida, J. (1982). "The Ends of Man." *Margins of Philosophy.* Chicago: The University of Chicago Press.

—. (1997). "The Theater of Cruelty and the Closure of Representation." *Mimesis, Masochism, & Mime: The Politics of Theatricality in Contemporary French Thought.* Ed. T. Murray. Ann Arbor: The University of Michigan Press: 40–62.

Dudley, J. M. (1992) "Being and Non-Being: The Other and Heterotopia in *Hamletmachine.*" *Modern Drama, 35* (4): 562–570.

Durkheim, E. (1915). *"Germany Above All": German Mentality and War.* Paris: A. Collin.

Elliston, D. (2004 November). "A Passion for the Nation: Masculinity, Modernity, and Nationalist Struggle." *American Ethnologist, 31*(4): 606–630.

Farren, G. (1833). *Essay on the Varities in Mania Exhibited by the Characters of Hamlet, Ophelia, Lear and Edgar.* London: Dean and Munday.

Feheravary, H (1976). "Enlightenment and Entanglement: History and Aesthetics in Bertolt Brecht and Heiner Müller." *New German Critique* 8: 80–109.

Fehrenbach, H. (1998). "Rehabilitating Fatherland: Race and German Remasculinization." *Signs.* 24 (1): 107–128.

Felman, S. (1975). "Women and Madness: The Critical Phallacy." *Feminisms: An Anthology of Literary Theory and Criticism.* Eds. R. R. Warhol and D. Price Herndl. New Brunswick: Rutgers University Press: 6-19.

Fink, C. & Hull, I. (1985). *German Nationalism and the European Response.* Norman: University of Oklahoma Press.

Flower, B. (1954). "The Drowned Girl. Rimbaud's 'Ophélie' and the German Literature." *GRM*: 108–119.

Foucault, M. (1988). *Madness and Civilization: A History of Insanity in the Age of Reason.* Trans. Richard Howard. New York: Vintage Books.

—. (1995). *Discipline and Punishment: The Birth of the Prison*. Trans. Alan Sheridan. New York: Vinatage Books.

Freud, S. (1961). "Femininity." *New Introductory Lectures On Psychoanalysis*. Trans. James Strachey. New York: W.W. Norton and Co.: 112-135.

Furness, H. H., Ed. (1877). *Hamlet, 1–2. A New Variorum Edition of Shakespeare*. London and Philadelphia: Lippincott: 3-4.

Guilfoyle, C. (1980). "'Ower Swete Sokor': The Role of Ophelia in Hamlet." *Comparative Drama* (14): 3-17. Reprinted in *Drama in the Renaissance: Comparative and Critical Essays* (1986). Ed. C. Davidson, C.J. Gianaaris, J.H. Stroupe. New York: AMS Press.

Gundolf, F. (1911). *Shakespeare und der deutsche Geist*. Berlin: Bondi.

Habicht, W. (1983). "Shakespeare in Nineteenth-Century Germany: The Making of a Myth." *Nineteenth-Century Germany: A Symposium*. Eds. Modris Eksteins and Hildegard Hammerschmidt. Tübingen: Gunter Narr Verlag: 141–157.

—. (1989). "Shakespeare and Theatre Politics in the Third Reich." *The Play Out of Context: Transferring Plays from Culture to Culture* Ed. H. Scolnicov and P. Holland. Cambridge: Cambridge University Press: 110-120.

—. (1992). "The Romanticism of the Schlegel-Tieck Shakespeare and the History of Nineteenth-Century German Shakespeare Translation." *European Shakespeares: Translating Shakepeare in the Romantic Age*. Trans. Lieven D'Hulst and Dirk Delabatista. Amsterdam: John Benjamin Publishing: 141–157.

Halpern, R. (1997). *"Hamletmachine." Shakespeare Among Moderns*). Ithaca: Cornell University Press: 227–288.

Hegel. G. W. F. (1975). *Aesthetics, 2*. Trans. T. Knox. Oxford, U.K.: Clarendon Press.

Heine, H. (1895). *Heine on Shakespeare: A Translation of His Notes on Shakespeare Heroines*. Trans. and Ed. Ida Benecke. Westminster: Archibald Constable and Co.

Hofacket, E. P. Jr. (1992). "Heiner Müller. *Dictionary of Literary Biography, 124*. Detroit: Gale Research: 333–346.

Hofele, A. (1992). "A Theatre of Exhaustion? 'Posthistoire' in Recent German Shakespeare Productions." *Shakespeare Quarterly, 43*(1): 80–86.

Homberg, A. (1988). "A Conversation with Robert Wilson and Heiner Müller. *Modern Drama, 31*(3): 454–458.

Hortmann, W. (1998). *Shakespeare on the German Stage*. Cambridge: Cambridge University Press.

Jeffords, S. (1998). "The 'Remasculinization' of Germany in the 1950s: Discussion." *Signs, 24*(1): 163–169.

Jones, H. A. (1916). *Shakespeare and Germany*. London: C. Whittingham and Co.

Kalb, J. (1995). "Müller and Mayakovsky." *Heiner Müller: ConTEXTS and HISTORY: A Collection of Essays from The Sydney German Studies Symposium 1994 'Heiner Müller/Theatre-History-Performance'*. Ed. Gerhard Fischer. Tubingen: Stauffenburg Verlag.

—. (1998a). "On Hamletmachine: Müller and the Shadow of Artaud." *New German Critique*, 73: 1–192.

—. (1998b). *The Theatre of Heiner Müller*. Cambridge: Cambridge University Press.

Kiefer, C. (2001). "The Myth and Madness of Ophelia." *The Myth and Madness of Ophelia.* Ed. Kiefer, C. Amherst: Mead Art Museum: pp. 11–39.

Klassen, J. (1986). "The Rebellion of the Body Against Ideas: Heiner Müller's Concept of Tragedy." *Within the Dramatic Spectrum.* Ed. K.V. Hartigan. Lanham, Maryland: University Press of America: 124–139.

Kozintzev, G. (1967). *Shakespeare: Time and Conscience*. Trans. Joyce Vining. London: Dennis Dobson.

Kromm, J. E. (1994). "The Feminization of Madness in Visual Representation." *Feminist Studies, 20*(3): 507–535.

Larson, K. (1988 March). "Did Shakespeare Really Write in German? Or: How the Bard Became *ein Klassiker*: Notes on the Politics of Culture." Unpublished paper presented to the Wells College Faculty Club.

—. (1991). "The Classical German Shakespeare as Emblem of Germany as 'geistige Weltmacht': Validating National Power through Cultural Prefiguration." Unpublished paper delivered at the 1991 Modern Language Association conference.

Leuca, G. (1955 November). "Wieland and the Introduction of Shakespeare into Germany." *The German Quaterly, 28*(4): 247–255.

Marinetti, F. T. (1909 February 20). "The Founding Manifesto of Futurism." *Le Figaro*. Paris: 86–89.

Minogue, V. (1989). "Rimbaud's Ophelia." *French Studies*, 43: 423–436.

Moeller, R. G. (1998). "The 'Remasculinization' of Germany in the 1950s: Introduction." *Signs, 24*(1): 101–106.

Mosse, G. L. (1982 April). "Friendship and Nationhood: About the Promise and Failure of German Nationalism." *Journal of Contemporary History. 17*(2): 351–367.

—. (1996). *The Image of Man: The Creation of Modern Masculinity.* New York: Oxford University Press.

—. (1985). *Nationalism and Sexuality: Respectability and Abnormal Sexuality in Modern Europe.* New York: H. Fertig.

Müller, H. (1984). *Hamletmachine and Other Texts for the Stage.* Ed. and Trans. Carl Weber. New York: Performing Arts Journal Publications.

—. (1995). "Shakespeare a Departure." Speech given the Shakespeare Festival in Weimar, 23 April, 1988. *Theatremachine.* Trans. and Ed. Marc von Henning. London: Faber & Faber: 99–102.

Mushcg, W. (1965). "Deutschland ist Hamlet." *Shakespeare Jahrbuch* (West): 32–58.

Nagele, R. (2002 December). "Phantom of a Corpse: Ophelia from Rimbaud to Brecht." *MLN, 117*(5): 1069–1082.

Pascal, R. (1937). *Shakespeare in Germany, 1740–1815.* Cambridge: The University Press.

Paulin, R. (2003). *The Critical Reception of Shakespeare in Germany 1682–1914. Native Literature and Foreign Genius.* Anglistische und Amerikanistische Texte und Studien 11. Hildesheim, Zurich, New York: Olms.

Pfister, M. (1986). "Germany is Hamlet: The History of a Political Interpretation." *New Comparison: A Journal of Comparative and General Literary Studies* 2: 106–126.

Phelan, P. (1993). *Unmarked.* New York: Routledge.

Rogoff, G. (1986). Review of *Hamletmachine* by H. Müller, R. Wilson (dir). *Performing Arts Journal,* 28: 54–57.

Rogowski, C. (1993). "Mad with Love: Medea in Euripides and Heiner Müller." *Themes In Drama 15: Madness in Drama.* Cambridge: Cambridge University Press: 171–182.

Ronell, A. (2004a). "Cutting Remarks." *Artforum, 11*(1): 30.

—. (2004b). "Deviant Payback: The Aims of Valerie Solanas." *SCUM Manifesto.* London: Verso.

Showalter, E. (1985). *The Female Malady: Women, Madness and English Culture 1830-1980.* New York: Pantheon Books.

—. (1985). "Representing Ophelia: Women, Madness, and the Responsibilities of Feminist Criticism." *Shakespeare and the Question of Theory.* Eds. Patricia Parker and Geoffrey Hartman. London: Methuen: 77-94.

Snyder, L. L. (1968). *The Meaning of Nationalism.* New York: Glenwood Press.

Solanas, V. (2004). *SCUM Manifesto.* With an introduction by Avital Ronell. London: Verso.

Teraoka, A. A. (1985). *The Silence of Entropy or Universal Discourse: The Postmoderninst Poetics of Heiner Müller*. New York: Peter Lang Publishing.

Walsh, B. (2001). "The Rest is Violence: Müller Contra Shakespeare." *Performing Arts Journal*, 69: 24-35.

Weber, C. (1980). "Heiner Müller: The Despair and the Hope." *Performing Arts Journal*, 4(3): 135-140.

—. (1984). "The Pressure of Experience." *Hamletmachine and Other Texts for the Stage*. Ed. and trans. Carl Weber. New York: *Performing Arts Journal Publications*: 13-30.

—. (2005). "Heiner Müller's Lysistrata Experiment." *Performance Arts Journal*, 27(1): 117–124.

Zimmermann, H. O. (1994). "Is Hamlet Germany? On the Political Reception of Hamlet." *New Essays on Hamlet*. Eds. Mark Thornton Burnett and John Manning. New York: AMS: 293–319.

Zizek, S. (1989). *The Subline Objective of Ideology*. London: Verso.

PART III

WAITING FOR HISTORY: MÜLLER AND THE DYNAMICS OF CULTURE AND POLITICS IN THE 21ST CENTURY

"What remains? Forsaken texts waiting on history."
—Heiner Müller, 1978

INTRODUCTION

In this our third and final section, our contributors take a look at the implications of Müller's work for the unfolding political and cultural dynamics of the new century.

Theatre is a temporal art forum. All playwrights write for a living audience, so it is no surprise that their work so often loses its relevance for future generations. Müller—who faced years when he had little or no prospect of being produced, with his acute sense of history and with his insistence on challenging the conventions of contemporary theatre— always seemed to have an eye on the future. His life's work, he said late in life, consisted of "forsaken texts waiting on history." (A quote that David Robinson borrows for the title of the first essay in this section, "Müller's 'Forsaken Texts Waiting on History' Find their American Moment.")

It is only a little over a decade since his death, so what "history" will do with Müller's "forsaken texts" remains to been seen. That said, a lot has changed—politically and culturally—since his death in 1995 and since the end of the Cold War, which, as Section I made clear, shaped so much of Müller's cultural politics. Given the collapse of communism, the virtually unchallenged (albeit perhaps brief) political, economic and cultural hegemony of the United States, the rise of religious-fueled terrorism and the expanding intellectual influence of postmodernism in the Western world, it seems reasonable to consider ourselves as living in a qualitatively different time than Müller. The scholars and artists contributing to this section, taking those changes as a given, consider Müller's work as important, if not more so, than it was during his own lifetime. However, they have different takes on that relevancy.

At least part of what underlies the differences between our contributors are different assumptions about the efficacy of theatre. Just how does a theatre performance—including a Müller performance—impact on/for/with its audience? It is a conversation that goes back as far as Aristotle and his notion of catharsis. The rise of realism and naturalism in 19th Century Europe brought with it the assumption/hope that exposing the audience to society's "reality" would lead to them wanting to change it. Ever since, there has been a tendency in the modern theatre to look for a utilitarian, directly political, use value for the theatre. Variations on this assumption were shared by realism, the agit-prop theatre of the 1920s and

'30s, and perhaps reached its most sophisticated rationale and level of practice in the work of Brecht and some of his contemporary followers, most notably Augusto Boal. A counter tendency—which has recently come to the fore due to postmodernism's understanding of reality itself as a social construct—has held that art in general and theatre in particular cannot be reduced to a cause-and-effect formula of any sort. Theatre at its best, this view holds, provides the audience with a unique (and hopefully provocative) experience, as much a part of creating reality as any other experience. An audience member will integrate that experience (or not) in an endless variety of ways.

David Robinson in "Müller's 'Forsaken Texts Waiting for History' Find their American Moment," and Joanne Taylor in "History in Fragments: The Brechtian Qualities of Müller's Late Dramaturgy," both approach Müller as an inheritor and developer of Brecht's utilitarian dramaturgy. Robinson, a former Secretary Treasurer of the International Brecht Society, reflects on his recent productions of Müller's *The Horatian* (1968) and *Mauser* (1970) with student performers at Georgia Southern University as Brechtian learning plays that have grown into American relevance post-9/11. Taylor argues that Müller's later dramaturgy is best understood as an adaptation of Brecht's concept of *Verfremdungseffekt*, which she translates (helpfully, I think) as "the process of making strange." She sees in Müller's "synthetic fragments" a continuation and intensification of Brecht's episodic structure, which "interrupts" the action on stage in order to make it strange, leading an ideal audience member to function as "a social, reflective and interactive participant."

On the other hand, David Kilpatrick in "After Ideology: Heiner Müller and the Theatre of Catastrophe" and Fred Newman in "Blooming Buzzing Confusion" both argue that Müller's importance lies precisely in his break with the political ideology and didactic dramaturgy of Brecht. Drawing parallels between Müller and the British playwright Howard Barker, Kilpatrick locates Müller's contemporary importance in his creation of a "post-ideological, post-theological drama, written for a theatre of catastrophe in which radical uncertainty violates any possibility of belief or opinion, much less truth." Newman sees in Müller's rejection in his later work of narrative and individuated character a "painful liberation from the constraints of ideology," a liberation that, Newman argues, challenges both the core aesthetic assumptions and the social function of the theatre as it has evolved over two and a half millennium. Thus, Newman writes, "Müller provides us not simply with new experiences, but with a new kind of experience." (While "Blooming Buzzing Confusion" is written by Newman and myself, its core ideas, which I wholeheartedly agree with, are original with Newman. My contribution lies primarily in placing those ideas within the broader context of theatre history.)

The differences over Müller's ongoing role in/impact on theatre and politics will obviously not be resolved here, nor can it be resolved, except, perhaps, on stages around the world. These chapters merely gesture toward a number of directions his influence may take.

Work Cited

Müller, Heiner (1978). "Producktiver Umgang mit Brecht. Ein Gespach." *Das Shauspielhaus.* Seitschrift des Hamburger Schausspiels, April-May: 85. Tran. David W. Robinson.

CHAPTER SIX

HISTORY IN FRAGMENTS: THE BRECHTIAN QUALITIES OF MÜLLER'S LATE DRAMATURGY

JOANNE TAYLOR

Four cots sit on a proscenium stage. Possibly army cots. Possibly in an interim army hospital. The cots are arranged parallel to one another in a neat row, their feet facing the audience. (A distorted mirroring of the Arlington cemetery.) Each cot is filled with a bandaged body. Male. White. Adorned in stained and torn fatigues. (Army hospital, indeed.) They speak: "Shall I speak of me I who / Do they speak of when / They speak of me I who is that."[1] These opening lines are pregnant with contemporary resonances: the speaker(s) is(are) enmeshed in a problem of knowing and articulating the self. The confusion of plurality—a first person singular multiple embodied—lends weight to the words spoken because we sense a shared solitude, which seeps into the audience. This weight increases with the unavoidable contemporary and historical resonances: the War in Iraq, the Vietnam War, UN "peace-keeping missions"/occupations, and so on.

With this mise-en-scène we find ourselves in Heiner Müller's fragmented performance text: *Landscape with Argonauts*. The actors are students at Mount Allison University in New Brunswick, Canada. The director is their professor Cordula Quint. The venue is the Castillo Theatre on 42nd Street in New York City. The occasion is a conference on "The Politics of Heiner Müller," organized by the Castillo Theatre in 2005. This text was originally published in 1982, as the third, and final, piece in a collection of motley play-fragments collectively titled *Verkommenes Ufer Medeamaterial Landschaft mit Argonauten (Depraved Shore Medeamaterial Landscape with Argonauts)*. The production and its occasion at the conference, where the differences between Brecht and Müller were emphasized, serves as a good jumping-off point for a discussion of the elements of continuity between Müller and his celebrated progenitor—a continuity that, I will argue, is essential to understanding the power and purpose of Müller's oeuvre.

The German dramatist and director Bertolt Brecht is most well-known for popularizing and developing Epic Theater, an approach first explored and named by his fellow German and fellow Marxist Erwin Piscador. Broadly speaking, Epic Theatre can be understood as an approach to theater-making that encourages active intellectual thought and decision-making on the part of both the artists involved and the audience members.

The basic elements of a Brechtian (or Epic) dramaturgy include: an episodic form; historical and cultural contextualization; the assumption of historical progress and theatrical efficacy/pedagogy; and active audience participation (at least intellectually if not physically). Epic Theater is one of a number of theatrical tendencies that rejected realism, (along with its "well-made-play" structure) in the first half of the 20th Century. Brecht, and his teacher Piscador, felt that realism could only show the surface of reality, not the social/economic and historical forces that produced that surface. The emotional empathy and over identification with particular characters engendered by realism got in the way, they maintained, of the audience's ability to get past the here-and-now to reflect on how the here-and-now came into being and might be changed. To break through the baggage of realism Brecht advocated, among other techniques, the use of titles (projected or otherwise) to describe the scene before it is performed, the refusal of theatrical illusion through the exposure of stage mechanics, and the use of song to break and comment on the action. Key to Brecht's dramaturgy—and key to understanding Müller's connection to it—is *der Verfremdungseffekt*. In the English-speaking world this is commonly known as the "alienation effect" thanks to John Willett's (in my opinion) mis-translation. Brecht's *Verfremdungseffekt* has little to do with either Marxist alienation, meaning a worker's lack of connectiveness to the product of her or his work in a capitalist economy, or to the popular psychological use of alienation, referencing an emotional state of discomfort and isolation from others. This last connotation of the word in English has led to a misunderstanding of Epic Theater as theater that is uncomfortably aloof, emotionally distant and overly cerebral. Michael Patterson proposes translating *der Verfremdungseffekt* as "distanciation" (Patterson, 274). Given that German puts words together to create new meaning far more frequently than we do in English, I think it more accurate (and helpful) to translate *Verfremdungseffekt* into the phrase "the process of making strange" (my translation). "This is not a mere linguistic quibble," Patterson points out, "for the word 'alienation' [in English] implies that audiences should become either antagonized by the performance or detached from the stage action to the point of boredom" (Patterson: 274).

Brecht called *der Verfremdungseffekt* a device "which prevents the audience from losing itself passively and completely in the character created by the actor, and which consequently leads the audience to be a consciously critical observer" (Brecht 1977: 91). The spectator is actively involved in the production, not from being cathartically sutured (to borrow a term from film studies) into the fictive world of theatrical illusion, but as a social, reflective and interactive participant. The process of making strange is, I believe, the core of Brecht's dramaturgy, that to which all its techniques are related and upon which its aesthetic/politic are based. Obviously it has implications for the actor's craft and it is in regard to acting that it is most often discussed. However, *der Verfremdungseffekt* has important implications for dramatic structure and dramatic language as well, and it is in this regard that we can most clearly link Brecht and Müller as artists.

Landscape with *Verbremdungseffekt*

Where does Müller fit within the historical trajectory of a Brechtian dramaturgy? His early plays, such as *Der Lohndrucker* (*The Scab*) (1956), were, as Carl Weber has put it, "written in the Epic mode Brecht had established" (Weber, 1984a: 16): with an episodic structure and characters embodying class and political types. It isn't until the early 1970s, with texts such as *Germania Death in Berlin* (1971), that Müller begins to move beyond the parameters of Epic Theatre as articulated (and staged) by Brecht. While many (including others in this collection) argue that Müller, in his mature works, moved away from the aesthetic and politics of Brechitan dramaturgy, to the point of considering, in Weber's words, "Brecht's 'theatre of enlightenment' an obsolete tool for the treatment of the complex reality of our age" (Weber, 1984a: 17). I argue to the contrary that Heiner Müller continues this important legacy in an unusual, though very appropriate, way. He takes Brecht on reluctantly and always with an eye to criticism and change. In Müller's own words, "To use Brecht without criticizing him is betrayal" (Müller 1990: 133). Müller is the Brechtian successor par excellence because he fits so uncomfortably in that role.

Let us now return to *Landscape with Argonauts*. The text was originally published in 1982, as the third, and final, piece in a collection of play fragments collectively titled *Verkommenes Ufer Medeamaterial*

Landschaft mit Argonauten (Depraved Shore Medeamaterial Landscape with Argonauts). Müller wrote each segment independently from the others, and each clearly functions as an autonomous text. The first, *Depraved Shore*, composed thirty years prior to its publication, "evokes East Berlin Suburbia with its lakes, commuter trains, housing developments, etc., a polluted landscape swarming with people whose minds are just as polluted" (Weber 1984b: 124). Fifteen years later Müller created *Medeamaterial*: a complex reworking of Euripides's *Medea* in which a woman betrays her family and country for the man she loves, and when he later casts her aside for a younger and more socially situated bride, Medea murders their sons both as a demonstration of her despair and as her revenge. In Müller's adaptation Medea speaks to her sons and husband, at times seeming to confuse them, in a stream-of-consciousness-style monologue. The closing fragment, *Landscape with Argonauts*, was written not long before its publication, and is a performance text without a speaker: it is a complex negotiation of locating the self in the mire of our postmodern world. Spanning a generation from initial creation to publication, these fragments serve as commentary on the processes of social and personal development within a fragmented postmodern world.

Depraved Shore Medeamaterial Landscape with Argonauts is an example of a form that Müller labeled the "synthetic fragment." First evident in *Germania Death in Berlin* (1971), this form represents, for many, the supposed shift from what Weber has called the "confinements of Brecht's model." In this new structure, seemingly "disparate scenes, or parts of scenes, are combined without any particular effort at a coherent, linear plot. The result is a kind of assemblage, much like a not yet fully structured work-in-progress." In fact, these synthetic fragments are actually "painstakingly crafted texts" (Weber 1984a: 17). Rather than viewing this shift as a break from Brecht, I see Müller's turn to the synthetic fragment as an evolution of Brecht, taking the process of making strange in new and powerful directions.

In his 1994 essay on *Mother Courage and Her Children*, bearing the same title as the play under consideration, Robert Leach outlines a schematic triad of Brecht's dramaturgy:

> Brecht wanted his theatre to intervene in the process of shaping society [...] (to over-schematize briefly) by a triad of *content* (better described in Brecht's case by the formalist term "material"), *form* (again the formalist term "technique" is more useful here), and *function*. In Brecht's dramatic form, these three constantly clash but never properly coalesce to compose a rounded whole. (Leach: 130)

In this triadic system the content, or material, is the gesture; the form, or technique, is the interruption of action; and the function is stimulation of the audience. The interruption of action is key to the overall formal structure and pedagogical conception of the Epic Theater—it is, on the structural level, *der Verfremdungseffekt*, that which makes the play strange. The gesture "has a definable beginning and a definable end," it is framed and circumscribed. Gestures are obtained by interrupting "someone engaged in an action," and the more often we interrupt, "the more gestures we obtain" (Benjamin 1973: 3). "The interruption therefore," Leach adds, serves, "as a means not only of pointing up something which a socialist realist play [or, I might add, any other realist play] would flow over, but pointing it up in such a way as to energize the spectator, to stimulate her or him into an awareness of the possibility for change." The power of the Epic Theater is the possibility it offers to the audience to recognize the potential for change and their agency in helping to effect that change. And this power, Leach writes, "derives precisely from the relationship between the material, the technique and the function, the 'gesture', the 'interruption' and the 'stimulation'" (Leach: 131).

A masterly example of this technique is to be found in scene ten in *The Life of Galileo* (1938/9), which opens with the following title: "During the next decade Galileo's doctrine spreads among the common people. Ballad-singers and pamphleteers everywhere take up the new ideas. In the carnival of 1632 many Italian cities choose astronomy as the theme for their guilds' carnival processions." This scene functions to interrupt the smooth, linear, chronological flow of the play's fictive-biographical narrative; through song it sums up the major intellectual actions of the play while, most importantly, commenting on attitudes within the diegetic space of the play, as well as those contemporaneous with Galileo, which mirror attitudes contemporary with Brecht. The song is performed by a "half-starved couple of fairground people with a baby and a five-year old girl," and the song itself criticizes not just the supposed absurdity of Galileo's theories, but the subsequent spectacle they engendered (Brecht 1994: 82). There are multiple layers of interruption: the play by the insertion of the song scene; the carnival by this "half-starved" family; the song by the Ballad Singer's own commentary; the Ballad Singer by his Wife; and their mini-performance by the carnival procession itself. The gesture of critical parody is the structuring material of this scene that serves as a comment on the material of the larger play as well as that of the play within its socio-historical moment (and hopefully the productions of the play within their socio-historical moments).

The Brechtian legacy in *The Scab*, Müller's first play, written the year of Brecht's death, is obvious. The play, which is set in a newly nationalized foundry in the German Democratic Republic (GDR) in 1948/9, consists of fifteen short scenes. It "presents the conflicts surrounding the attempts of a 'model worker' and activist, Balke, to improve productivity and develop innovative practices in restoring the furnaces of the damaged and run-down plant so that it can contribute to post-war recovery" (Milfull). The characters embody various social types. Rather than presenting an attempted solution, the play, according to Müller, "tries to carry the struggle ['between the Old and the New'] into the new audience who will decide it" (Müller, 1989: 28). Gestures are circumscribed: Stettiner throwing a cigarette, Geschke picking-up the cigarette; the act of playing cards; manicuring; the paying out of wages; laying bricks. The fragmentary quality of the scenes speaks to their interruption: no chance for thorough development or follow-through.

The Brechtian nature of *Depraved Shore Medeamaterial Landscape with Argonauts* is, on first encounter, less obvious. Weber has described its "dramatic structure, or rather, anti-structure," as "post-structuralist" or "deconstructionist" (Weber 1984a: 17). We might then read the Brechtian episodic form as "structuralist" or even "constructionist." Reducing the Brecht-Müller relationship to such a simple mode of linear association, to a dichotomy of structure verses post-structure misses the point. It also misses the fact that Müller's later work is very well structured, and the structure is a new way of carrying on the process of making strange through interruption.

The structure of the synthetic fragment is the Brechtian interruption taken to a new level (or in a new direction). The text interrupts itself, each fragment an interruption of the others. Their impact is realized through their juxtaposition. Brecht's episodic scenes become Müller's scenic fragments: the sense of disruption between scenes is intensified. In the work under consideration, written over a period of decades, we might assume that the apparent fragmented interruption between scenes marks their discontinuous relationship. Rather, their fragment-like structure serves as a mode of gestic interruption: we view each scene as its own complete gesture, it is marked and self-contained. The action of the scene is pointed up "in such a way as to stimulate the spectator" (Leach: 131). The first fragment, *Depraved Shore*, serves as a set of stage directions in which the mise-en-scène is described. *Medeamaterial* becomes the "expected" play with characters, dialogue, and action. *Landscape with Argonauts*, then, is the coda or epilogue: here, the author speaks directly out of the work commenting on his text, on his text's cultural position, as well as his own. Whereas Brecht, through a formal structuring of scenes, creates a larger text using positive, dialectical construction (narrative), Müller's texts are constructed in more negative terms with the scenes/fragments in discursive tension, almost fighting each other rather than working together.

Conflict, then, for Müller, becomes a necessary element of interruption, or even the dramaturgical technique that replaces interruption. "I believe in conflict, I don't believe in anything else. What I try to do in my writings is to strengthen the sense of conflicts, to strengthen confrontations and contradictions. There is no other way. I'm not interested in answers and solutions. I don't have any to offer. I'm interested in problems and conflicts" (Müller 1990: 34). The dialectics of Müller's dramaturgy function through conflict—not primarily, as in earlier theatre (including Brecht's), through conflict between characters within the context of a narrative, but conflict between the various parts of the text/performance. To use Leach's terms, the form/technique itself is the play's conflict. Weber quotes Müller as suggesting that all three parts of the text are "happening simultaneously" (Weber 1984b: 125), a staging that would heighten the suggested conflict: each scene would be competing for the audience's attention; each fighting with the other on the level of mise-en-scène, staging, costume, etc.

Making Language Strange

Of course, conflict in Müller's later texts occurs not just at the level of inter-scene, but intra-scene as well. Müller presents a conflict of voices, suggesting the struggle of individuality with/within a collectivist state. This conflict of voices is most apparent in the visual construction of the text:

Lake near Straussberg Depraved shore Traces
Of flatheaded Argonauts
Reedbristles Dead branches
THIS TREE WILL OUTGROW ME Fish corpses
Glisten In the mud Boxes of cookies Piles of shit
FROMMS ACT CASINO
The torn menstrual pads The blood
Of the women of Colchis
BUT YOU MUST BE CAREFUL *JA*
YES YES YES YES
DIRTY CUNT I SAY TO HER THAT IS MY MAN
PENETRATE ME COME SWEETS
The Argo smashes the skull into him The useless

Ship
That hangs in the tree Hangar and shitroom
The vulture surveillance point

These are the opening lines to *Depraved Shore*, which, according to the author's note, "...can be performed in the current business of a Peepshow." The suggested setting allows for the possibility of multiple voices isolated in their individual rooms: they are speaking with one another in the sense that each speaks on top of the other, but they are not speaking *to* one another. The voices overlap, almost unaware of the other, yet each is part of and contributing to a generalized landscape: a place strung with detritus, which is the materialization of a decaying sociality. The phrases butt up against one another: "Lake near Strassberg Depraved shore Traces / Of flatheaded Argonauts." The first line consists of more than two phrases, but not quite three because the third is interrupted by a line break. This interruption forces us to linger on the word "traces" (*Spur*). In the original German, the word carries on like an idling machine or the running of water; in English, it enacts that which calls forth by leaving audible remnants of itself in the air. The phrasing continues in this fashion, cramming multiple phrases into one line, forcing each phrase into literal combat against another for space, while at the same time rendering other phrases asunder by quickly moving to the next line. These phrasal voices are then interrupted by a new voice, as represented in the text by all caps. This voice is intrusive, it is loud (not necessarily in volume), it pulls focus (what little focus there may have been), and it suggests a schizophrenic clash of competing thoughts.

As the text moves to the next fragment, *Medeamaterial*, we experience a shift not just of voice but also of narrative style: from the confused stream-of-consciousness to a more standard dramatic format with characters and dialogue. In this fragment Medea confronts Jason, at times confusing him and her sons—a subtle difference between second person singular and plural not readily apparent in English—lamenting her position as both betrayer and betrayed. Müller provides three characters—Medea, Jason, and the Nurse—and thus three distinct voices; but this is not where the conflict lies. Rather, the conflict lies within Medea herself: here we witness an internal conflict as she struggles with who she has become, what she has done, how she arrived at her current position, and what she must do (ultimately, murder her sons). There is a battle over to whom she is speaking:

And my brother My brother Jason
Who I threw in the path of your pursuers

Cut-up by these my sister hands
To aid your flight from the robbed father
Of my and his body you your sons
Do you want them back your sons
You owe me a brother Jason
Who do you love more the dog or the bitch

In this last line the "you" has shifted from singular to plural (from the German "*du*" to "*ihr*"). From here Medea moves back and forth between addressing Jason and addressing her sons. The tension of addressees is much more apparent in the English text because of the lack of distinction between second person singular and plural, we are often left behind when this shift occurs, causing a confusion of focus and intent. As reader and spectator we are inducted into the text and become un/willing objects of address. In this way Müller is able to draw the spectator into the work, making her a dramatic participant.

Language provides Müller with another mode of "making strange"— the use of foreign language in the text. In the third, and final, fragment, *Landscape with Argonauts*, Müller inserts a spattering of English phrases. With this third fragment, we have a return to *Depraved Shore* in terms of voice-conflict, as evidenced in the tension of phrasing as well as the use of phrases in all caps:

I cud of a man I cud
Of a woman Platitude upon platitude I dream-hell
That wears my chance-name I anxiety
Before my chance-name
MY GRANDFATHER WAS
AN IDIOT IN BOEOTIA
I my sea voyage
I my stolen land My
Walk through the suburbs I my death

Structurally this is quite similar to *Depraved Shore*; in fact the two seem like mirror images flanking the dramatic *Medeamaterial*. There are a few subtle differences, however: Müller does not provide any stanza breaks; this fragment is a single, uninterrupted flow of language, echoing Medea's speech.

While *Landscape* does recall *Depraved*, the similarities between the first and third fragments are interrupted with the insertion of English. The German text reads:

ODER DIE GLÜCKLOSE LANDUNG Die toten Neger

Wie Pfähle in den Sumpf gerammt
In den Unifromen ihrer Feinde
DO YOU REMEMBER DO YOU NO I DON'T
Das getrocknete Blut
Qualmt in der Sonne

The disruptive shift in language is apparent, and I would argue important, but the prominent published translations (Weber and Marc von Henning) leave this line in English. [2] Doing so misses the point: Müller is interested in conflict at many levels, including that of language. Being a prominent East German playwright, Müller often struggled with the ideological problem of the growing dominance of capitalism, particularly the type of capitalism circulated by the United States. In this line—"DO YOU REMEMBER DO YOU NO I DON'T"—we have a question, its shortened repetition, and a response. The urgency of the questioning suggests interrogation, while the demand for remembering alludes to the conflicted German relationship to World War II. The conflict of language exists at many levels: the jarring disruption of familiarity, of being able to understand what is being said; the conflict of one's relationship to their troubled past; and the conflict of voices/speakers. In order to maintain this layering of tension I propose an alternate translation:

OR THE UNLUCKY LANDING The dead negroes
Like posts rammed into the marsh
In the uniforms of their enemies
ERRINNERT IHR EUCH ERINNERT NEIN ICH ERRINERE MICH
NICHT
The dried blood
Smoked in the sun

The English-speaking reader/spectator experiences a similar interruption of language, having momentarily lost their way along the dramatic path laid out by Müller.

If Brecht's technique of interruption (form) becomes Müller's conflict, what happens to the gestic material (content) and spectatorial stimulation (function)? The synthetic fragment form seems to be a response to the fragmented experience of postmodern life (see: Jameson's linguistic islands); and the "pressure of experience" is, for Müller, "a pre-condition of writing" (Weber 1984a: 15). For Müller this is the experience of a divided Germany, a divided history, and a divided subjectivity. Brecht's episodic form was the result of a systematized relationship to, and ordering of, content; and this content was itself a premeditated comment on current socio-political events and conditions. Brecht was interested in engendering and participating in a structured, progressive dialogue that would lead to positive social change. With Brecht we can discern a moral and direct purpose. Brecht the didact. For Müller, this certainty evaporates with the shaken, German ground on which he stands. Müller also desires dialogue, but rather than coming from a clearly defined position he allows the confusion of experience to take form on the page and stage. He doesn't have an answer, nor presumes that one exists: conflicting fragments replace coherent narration.

Making Experiences Possible

If *der Verfremdungseffekt* is, indeed, at the dramaturgical core of Müller's mature work, the question must be asked: toward what end? The last fifty years has seen the adoption of many of Brecht's theatrical techniques by the mainstream theatres of Europe and the United States. However, separated from their political context, these techniques have become just that—new aesthetic technique, an interesting trick. How many productions today expose the lighting and other stage mechanics? Yet how many of those productions are about engendering thought? Technique torn from its relationship with political/historical content and its revolutionary function is neutered technique.

One can hardly charge Müller with neutering *der Verfremdungseffekt.* Müller is like the Bible; you can find within his canon of interviews, essays and texts for the stage quotes to justify a wide range of seemingly contradictory political and aesthetic viewpoints. That said, given his choice to stick with the GDR until the end (discussed elsewhere in this volume) and the historical/political content of his texts, it seems irrefutable that he considered himself a political writer and wanted his plays to impact/interact with society in a progressive way. Müller's development of Brecht's *der Verfremdungseffekt*, was, for him, never simply an aesthetic exploration (although it was that too); it was a political engagement of his audience and his political environment.

To explore this, let us continue with our examination of *Depraved Shore Medeamaterial Landscape With Argonauts.* The totality of the author's note to the text already referenced, reads:

> The text needs the naturalism of the set. DEPRAVED SHORE can be performed in the current business of a Peepshow, MEDEAMATERIAL by a sea at Straussberg that is a muddy swimming pool in Beverly Hills or the public baths of a mental hospital. Just like MAUSER represents society at the edge, LANDSCAPE WITH ARGONAUTS represents the catastrophes that mankind is working toward. The landscape could be dead stars, on

which a search party from another time or another place hears a voice and finds a corpse. Like every landscape the I in this section is collective. The three sections can be performed simultaneously.

As the note makes clear, Müller is interested in the ways in which theatre can be used to "intervene" on daily life. His position on the nature of this intervention is more ambiguous than Brecht's. Brecht's content, form and function all centered around didacticism. The implicit assumption of his work is that he (the author) knows the answer/the way/the method and is working to find ways to help the audience learn what the playwright knows. Brecht's efforts to help the audience think/reflect assumes that if an individual (or audience or social class) understands what is really going on they will, as a result, act in accordance with that understanding. Müller does not share Brecht's faith in rationalism. For Müller individuals have become so alienated and social classes so disconnected from their presumed historical tasks, that the ability to do anything growthful or transformative at all is in question. For Müller drama is not so much the transmission of knowledge anymore, but, "the task of making experiences possible" (qtd. in Brenner: 24). So, while for Brecht (and some of his followers such as Augusto Boal) the model remains the classroom, for Müller theatre, at its best, is, rather a "laboratory of social imagination" (qtd. in Brenner: 34).

A laboratory, none-the-less, is involved in inquiry and has the potential to make discoveries that impact on the larger society. We can see in the image of the laboratory a continuation of Brecht's dramaturgy to the extent that it is interested in interfacing and influencing contemporary political and cultural situations. Müller, like Brecht, is interested in the ways that theater can be used to intervene on history—and, as with his mentor, the primary method of that intervention, as we have seen, is through *der Verbrendungseffekt*. As he wrote of *Despoiled Shore Medeamaterial Landscape with Argonauts*: "...it presumes the catastrophes which mankind is working toward. The theatre's contribution to their prevention can only be their representation" (Weber 1984a: 14).

As much as Müller may have denied ideology and claimed no political intent in his writing, we cannot deny his important political position—a position that he may have been thrust into (arguable) but one that he seemed to embrace if not enjoy (and definitely take advantage of) as is apparent by the number of interviews, talks, visits, etc. that he did throughout his artistic life. Even if his writing was purely selfish, as he sometimes claimed, it comes from a self that was fully enmeshed in a political world—and as Althusser would argue, we are all already ideological subjects. Also, as is evident from the numerous interviews,

Müller was very politically aware and theoretically well versed, and in this, too, he was walking in Brecht's footsteps.

It seems undeniable that Müller, like Brecht, was a political playwright who built on Brecht's "process of making strange" to approach playwriting as political (even revolutionary) activity. His difference with Brecht was not one of political commitment but a result of the different times in which they lived. David Barnett sums it up well:

> Müller is forced to deal with politics in such a questioning way because of the great historical defeats that socialism has sustained this century. The failure of the Soviet experiment and more particularly the GDR has demanded a new political discourse in the theatre. Müller is very much interested in the future of Marxism ... but it is a future which has to submit itself to ruthless (self-)examination in order to have a future. (Barnett: 250)

Müller's later dramaturgy is, thus, a process of making strange (and unacceptable) the creeping political and cultural stasis that brought communism to an end and keeps the world spinning its wheels on a dead-end street.

Notes

[1] All translations of this text, originally published in German as *Verkommenes Ufer Medeamaterial Landschaft mit Argonauten* (1982), are mine unless otherwise noted.
[2] Carl Weber: "OR THE HAPLESS LANDING The dead negroes / Rammed into the swamp like poles / In the uniforms of their enemies / DO YOU REMEMBER DO YOU NO I DON'T / The fried up blood / Is smoking in the sun" (1984: 135). Marc von Henning: "OR THE UNHAPPY LANDING The dead negroes / Hammered into the moor like stakes / Dressed in the uniforms of their enemies / DO YOU REMEMBER DO YOU NO I DON'T / The coagulated blood / Is billowing in the sun" (1995: 56)

Work Cited

Barnett, David (1998). *Literature versus Theatre: Textual problems and theatrical realization in the later plays of Heiner Müller*. Bern: Peter Lang.

Benjamin, Walter (1968). "Theses on the Philosophy of History." *Illuminations*. Edited by Hannah Arendt. Trans. Harry Zohn. New York: Harcourt Brace: 253-264.

—. (1973). *Understanding Brecht*. Trans. Anna Bostock. London: NLB.

Brecht, Bertolt (1977). "Introductory Note." In *The Measures Taken and Other Lehrstücke*. Trans. Carl R. Mueller. New York: Arcade Publishing.

—. (1994). *The Life of Galileo*. Translated by John Willett. Edited by John Willett and Ralph Manheim. New York: Arcade Publishing.

Brenner, Eva (1994). "HAMLETMACHINE Onstage: A Critical Analysis of Heiner Müller's Play in Production." *DAI 55*: New York University.

Fehervary, Helen (1976). "Enlightenment or Entanglement: History and Aesthetics in Bertolt Brecht and Heiner Müller." *New German Critique*. 8: 80-109.

Leach, Robert (1994). "*Mother Courage and Her Children*." *Cambridge Companion to Brecht*. Eds. Peter Thomson and Glendyr Sacks. Cambridge: Cambridge University Press: 128-138.

Milfull, John.
http://www.litencyc.com/php/sworks.php?rec=true&UID=14462

Müller, Heiner (1984). *Hamletmachine. Hamletmachine and Other Texts for the Stage*. Ed. and trans. Carl Weber. New York: Performing Arts Journal Publications: 49-58.

—. (1989). *The Scab* In *The Battle: Plays, Prose, Poems by Heiner Müller*. Ed. and trans. Carl Weber. New York: Performing Arts Journal Publications: 23-56.

—. (1990). *Germania*. Trans. by Bernard and Caroline Schütze. Ed. by Sylvère Lotringer. New York: Seimotext(e).

—. (1995). *Waterfront Wasteland Medea Material Landscape with Argonauts. Theatremachine*. Ed. and trans. Marc von Henning. Boston: Faber and Faber: 45-58.

Patterson, Michael (1994). "Brecht's Legacy." *Cambridge Companion to Brecht*. Eds. Peter Thomson and Glendyr Sacks. Cambridge: Cambridge University Press: 273-287.

Roddy, Jr., Harry Louis (2000). "A Revolutionary Critique of Individualism: Heiner Müller's *Mauser*." *Monatshefte* 92: 184-198.

Weber, Carl (1980). "Heiner Müller: The Despair and the Hope." *Performing Arts Journal* 4: 135-140.

—. (1984a). "The Pressure of Experience." *Hamletmachine and Other Texts for the Stage*. Ed. and trans. Carl Weber. New York: Performing Arts Journal Publications: 13-30.

—. (1984b). Introductory Note to *Despoiled Shore Medeamaterial Landscape with Argonauts. Hamletmachine and Other Texts for the Stage*. Ed. and trans. Carl Weber. New York: Performing Arts Journal Publications: 124-125.

—. (1989). Introductory Note to *The Scab. The Battle: Plays, Prose, Poems by Heiner Müller*. Ed. and trans. Carl Weber. New York: Performing Arts Journal Publications: 23-24.

CHAPTER SEVEN

MÜLLER'S "FORSAKEN TEXTS WAITING FOR HISTORY" FIND THEIR AMERICAN MOMENT

DAVID W. ROBINSON

In 1988, when I was living in Berlin on a Fulbright Fellowship to the German Democratic Republic (GDR), I participated in a seminar on Heiner Müller led by Frank Hörnigk, Humboldt University's noted advocate of contemporary GDR literature. A longtime defender of progressive and politically independent East German writers, Hörnigk was a maverick within the Communist Party who eight years earlier had withstood a vicious disciplinary proceeding on charges of counterrevolutionary conspiracy. The Müller seminar was therefore a politically ambiguous event at a time when the reactionary East German regime was flailing wildly in response to Mikhail Gorbachev's reform initiatives in the Soviet Union. The composition of the seminar was also unusual; in addition to a dozen East German students, there were participants from the Soviet Union, France, Spain, Japan, and two from the United States. An atmosphere open to politically charged issues emerged, though with odd distortions resulting from the foreign visitors' quasi-ambassadorial status within an East German milieu.

This was not the first internationally-inflected discussion of Müller that had occurred, of course, inasmuch as he had enjoyed a vogue in West Germany and New York for some years, but it was the first time that such a discussion had taken place inside the German Democratic Republic. The questions raised were framed in a distinctively East German way: we approached the plays in light of the issues of GDR history, socialist identity, and revolutionary consciousness that turn up consistently as Müller's favored themes.

This constellation of people and circumstances (foreign readers confronting Müller not as a member of an international avant-garde, but as an East German writer struggling with East German history and identity) generated some interesting questions that bear on the general topic of Müller's continuing significance in America. I recall that Hörnigk frequently turned to me and asked–in the midst of some abstruse discussion of revolutionary praxis–how I would apply these ideas to circumstances in the United States. I generally had no answer. This essay begins to frame an answer (19 years late) by seeking a continuum between my experiences in that seminar room and my current experience of teaching Müller's plays to American undergraduate literature majors. At the East German end of this continuum we had the efforts of socialist writers, situated within an oppressive, intellectually constricted regime in the eastern camp of the Cold War, to depict history truthfully and to visualize the New Socialist Man or Woman; at the other end, in early 21st century America, we face the unfettered hegemony of globalized capital coupled with the historical singularity of 9/11 and the so-called War on Terror it has underwritten. Müller's rigor in addressing one historical moment offers a key to addressing our own amid historical amnesia and reckless imperialism.

First, then, two points about East German literary history. The first concerns Bertolt Brecht. Brecht's return to Germany in 1949 and his leadership at the Berliner Ensemble until his death in 1956 set the pattern for all East German theater that followed. It would be Marxist in conviction, austerely detached in performance style, and frankly didactic in its social engagement. In its rejection of realism and its embrace of stylized, symbolic representation and other earmarks of the early 20th century theatrical avant-garde, Brecht's theater maintained a living connection with the vigorous experimental theater of Weimar Germany. [1]

Yet despite Brecht's revered status, his East German theatrical and literary successors differed from him sharply and consistently in a crucial respect: the importance of history in their works. For Brecht, more often than not, history is just one alienation technique among others, a warehouse of exotic props that not even Brecht takes very seriously. The settings of *The Good Person of Szechuan* or *The Caucasian Chalk Circle* (like that of *The Winter's Tale*, with its Bohemian seacoast) are little more than neutral fairy-tale landscapes whose rather off-hand use provides an undistracted view of the ethical issues and social conflicts in the plays. Like ideology, Brecht's plots take place outside of history. [2] Social processes are dissected, but their historical development is not investigated. Consciousness means analysis of material reality in the here and now. This ahistorical dimension is even more evident in the expressly didactic teaching plays, such as *The Measures Taken*, with its repeated invocation of a scriptural "ABC of communism" (Brecht: 11, 13, 34), its anti-illusionistic staging, constant exchanging of roles, overt mask symbolism, and evident roots in the Noh drama. The Young Comrade's single task is to suppress his humanitarian impulses when they conflict with Marxist doctrine or Party discipline. Memory is not a factor in any sense beyond his repeated failure to remember his instructions or even his past failures. His consciousness is an academic consciousness, failing or passing a series of tests, instead of a consciousness conditioned by a past or by the need to reconcile a catastrophic past with an uncertain present. In Brecht, there is no past, and the future is a communist millennium distantly glimpsed. To Müller, indeed, writing in 1977 to theater director Reiner Steinweg, Brecht's teaching plays seemed somewhat dated as models for an engaged theater, having emerged from a historical caesura between the two wars and bound to the revolutionary praxis of a now-distant period:

> I think that we need to take leave of the teaching play until the next earthquake comes. The Christian End Time of *The Measures Taken* has run its course, history has adjourned the tribunal in the streets, and the learned chorus has ceased to sing, humanism manifests itself only as terrorism, the Molotov cocktail is the final bourgeois learning experience. What remains: forsaken texts waiting for history. And the moth-eaten memory, the crumbling wisdom of the masses, always threatened by forgetfulness. (Müller 1978: 85) [3]

In contrast to Brecht, but in common with many other GDR writers of his generation (most notably Christa Wolf), Müller's consciousness was defined by the serial cataclysms of fascism, German military defeat, and imposed socialism. The classic Brechtian teaching play—full of revolutionary optimism and equipped with a clear outcome, seemed less than relevant amid the deadlocked nuclear terror of the Cold War and with Stalinist terror a recent memory. Müller's revolutionary protagonists never escape a split sense of time and responsibility: they are themselves the antagonists to be defeated, their present selves a synthesis of guilty memory and unfolding crisis.

From this personal and generational experience of revolutionary turmoil ending in precarious historical deadlock (what Müller imagined as an "Ice Age" in *Hamletmachine* [Müller 1984: 58]) follows a second significant fact of literary history: that the central cultural project of GDR literature in its mature period was the redefinition of the socialist *Menschenbild*, that is, of the definition of the "human" under socialism. The topos of the New Socialist Man originates, of course, in Marx's vision of a classless communist polity that frees human creativity from the realm of necessity, as expressed in *The German Ideology*:

> [A]s soon as the distribution of labour comes into being, each man has a particular, exclusive sphere of activity, which is forced upon him and from which he cannot escape. He is a hunter, a fisherman, a herdsman, or a critical critic, and must remain so if he does not want to lose his means of livelihood; while in communist society, where nobody has one exclusive sphere of activity, but each can become accomplished in any branch he wishes, society regulates the general production and thus makes it possible for me to do one thing today and another tomorrow, to hunt in the morning, fish in the afternoon, rear cattle in the evening, criticize after dinner, just as I have a mind, without ever becoming hunter, fisherman, herdsman or critic. (Marx and Engels, *The German Ideology*: I, A, 4)

The New Socialist Man preoccupies early Soviet literature and takes a classic form in the novels of Fyodor Gladkov and Nikolai Ostrovsky, which feature resolute communist heroes struggling to overcome their private weaknesses and desires so as to better serve the cause of socialism. The decadent period may be said to set in with the politico-aesthetic dogma of Socialist Realism enunciated in 1934 by Stalin's cultural-political mouthpiece, A. A. Zhdanov:

> Comrade Stalin has called our writers engineers of human souls. What does this mean? What duties does the title confer upon you?
> In the first place, it means knowing life so as to be able to depict it truthfully in works of art, not to depict it in a dead, scholastic way, not simply as "objective reality," but to depict reality in its revolutionary development.
> In addition to this, the truthfulness and historical concreteness of the artistic portrayal should be combined with the ideological remolding and education of the toiling people in the spirit of socialism. This method in *belles lettres* and literary criticism is what we call the method of socialist realism. (Zhdanov)

In this formulation, and despite the seemingly historical and dialectical sound of "revolutionary development," Marx's utopianism was replaced by a rigid taxonomy of character completely alien to open-ended exploration of human experience under changed social conditions, an enlivening dynamism that was present in the work of Gladkov, for instance. The orthodoxy of Socialist Realism persisted as official GDR cultural policy into the 1970s.[4]

Beginning around 1960, however, and accelerating after the building of the Berlin Wall in 1961, GDR writers with various degrees and styles of commitment to socialism began to reclaim and redefine the socialist *Menschenbild*. The GDR had been in existence for a decade; fascism had been defeated for nearly two decades. The labor-force hemorrhage caused by emigration had been stanched by the closing of the Berlin border, bringing economic stability and (perforce) a turning-inward of national attention. Official government policy was to regard the current moment, circa 1961, as the dawn in the GDR of "really existing socialism," as opposed to the prospective or merely utopian kind. (Of course, this formulation was a way of euphemistically side-stepping socialism's all-too-evident failings.) In the official literary historiography of the period, this social transformation ushered in a distinctive *Ankunftsliteratur* (literature of arrival) that concerned itself with the daily experience and continuing advances of achieved socialism, viewed primarily from the perspective of politically-engaged young people.[5]

Indeed, a generation imbued with socialist ideals had come of age under social conditions markedly different from those of West Germany. Novelists including Christa Wolf, Uwe Johnson, Hermann Kant, Erwin Strittmatter, and, somewhat later, Ulrich Plenzdorf and Christoph Hein, began creating narratives and characters that in large part preserved the categories and pieties of Socialist Realism while bringing a much more critical spirit to bear on its underlying assumptions and didactic intent. A motif of particular interest is the missing or impossible hero in the novels of these writers. The narratives open with a literally or figuratively dead protagonist, and then unfold retrospectively as an attempt by a narrator to make sense of the protagonist's death and its meaning to GDR society. In the older, paradigmatic Socialist Realist plot, the protagonist confronts and defeats careerist Party bureaucrats, counter-revolutionaries, and his own personal doubts and human weaknesses to ultimately achieve an advanced level of class consciousness and to prevail in the struggle for socialism. In the revised, 1960s version, though in general the larger project survives and moves forward, the socialist hero endures irremediable personal tragedy and even failure. These novels may be read as thought experiments putting to the test the regime's claims of having achieved a just and prosperous socialism. In other words, if exemplary and committed characters are stymied, ostracized, worn down, and destroyed by the machinery of contemporary GDR society, what does this say about the society? The writers involved in rethinking the stock *Menschenbild* were broadly acknowledging the difficulty of achieving both personal fulfillment and an ethical social profile in the GDR (a problem usually laid at the door of the demonized West). Moving beyond fervent revolutionary clichés, what did it mean *now* to be a socialist? And what did it mean to be

a human being now that socialism had putatively been achieved? Which is
no more than to ask: What is the right way to live, and (as Brecht would
have added) is it compatible yet with personal happiness?

Now back to the East Berlin seminar in 1988. Frank Hörnigk's
approach to Müller blends the two dominant East German themes I have
been describing: the specificity of addressing a particular history (in this
case, the history of German socialism under Soviet domination) through
the lens of its implications and its consequences for individuals.
Furthermore, the questions raised are eminently practical—they are ethical
questions that arise for individuals committed to acting in accord with
abstract principles, in this case, a Marxist vision of social justice. Müller
characteristically seeks out the moment of crisis when these two
considerations, the awareness of the past and the ethical demands of the
present, come into sharpest conflict. Borrowing from Walter Benjamin,
Hörnigk describes this tension between awareness of past catastrophe and
present ethical action as a process of *Eingedenken*, which means
approximately "mindfulness" or "remembrance" or "memorialization."
Benjamin was addressing the question (which he quotes here from Max
Horkheimer) of whether history must be viewed as closed or open—a
question ultimately of free will and the possibility of escaping historical
determination:

> "The assertion [Horkheimer says] that history is open is idealistic if it does
> not include in itself the notion of finality. The injustices of the past did
> happen and they are final. The victims of murder really were murdered . . .
> To take openness completely seriously you would have to believe in the
> Last Judgment . . . there arises perhaps in connection with openness a
> distinction between the positive and the negative, so that injustice, terror,
> the pain of the past are irreparable. Justice, joy, deeds appear in a different
> light in the present because their positive character is largely negated by
> the past. This applies above all to individual existence, in which not
> happiness but unhappiness is confirmed by death." The corrective to this
> line of reasoning lies in the consideration that history is not merely a
> science but also a form of remembrance [*Eingedenken*]. What science has
> asserted, remembrance can modify. Remembrance can change the open
> (happiness) to the final and the final (suffering) to the open. This is
> theology, but in remembrance we discover something that forbids us to
> grasp history in a fundamentally a-theological way, however much we may
> seek to avoid using directly theological concepts. (Benjamin 1982: 588-
> 589)

By "theological" Benjamin may be understood as invoking an
essentially ungrounded moral claim, here perceived in the activity (a

central one in Jewish tradition) of remembering the dead and
acknowledging one's connectedness and responsibility to them. The
meaning becomes clearer when applied to the bloody history of Marxist
revolution, with its roots in Leninist terror and its ultimate self-immolation
in Stalinist madness. Müller's work is one of the GDR's most vigorous
efforts to understand the continuing meaning of Stalinism, especially its
effect on contemporary ethical actions taken in the name of justice or
liberation. The long and repetitive list of violent events in the name of
socialism, some criminal and some justified, must be born in mind today
by every engaged socialist; as Müller put it in 1972, "The more socialism
comes to determine the course of history, the more important it is to
remember what it has cost" (quoted in Hörnigk 1990: 132).

Hörnigk cites Müller's 1958 "Hapless Angel" fragment (itself based on
Benjamin's "Angel of History"[6]) as a key to understanding the process of
Eingedenken that informs the plays, balancing the paralyzing weight of
history against the continued necessity of action:

> THE HAPLESS ANGEL. A flood accumulates behind him, scattering
> debris on his wings and shoulders, with a noise of buried drums, while
> before him the future rises, presses on his eyes, explodes the eyeballs like a
> star, twists words into loud gagging, strangles him with its breath. For a
> time his wing-beats still can be seen, the roar of stones heard falling before
> or behind him, the vain movements now loud as he struggles, now isolated
> and slowing. Then the moment closes over him: quickly covered by debris,
> the hapless angel comes to rest, waiting for history in the petrifaction of
> flight gaze breath. Until the renewed roar of mighty wing-beats propagates
> in waves through the stone and announces his flight. (Müller 1998: 53)

Müller's metaphor captures the dangerous stasis of the Cold War while
anticipating the "next earthquake" of history and the resumption of a
stalled revolution. In his most important dramatization of this, *The Task*,
Müller develops the angel motif further, transforming it into the Angel of
Despair, a paradoxical figure embodying both the forgetfulness of history
and its resumption in the future out of the depths of misery:

> I am the Angel of Despair. With my hands I dispense ecstasy, numbness,
> oblivion, the lust and the torment of bodies. My language is silence, my
> song the scream. . . . I am the knife with which the dead man cracks open
> his coffin. I am the one who will be. My flight is the rebellion, my sky the
> abyss of tomorrow. (Müller 1984: 87)

Hörnigk argues that Müller's teaching plays (among others)
demonstrate precisely this memorialization of the dead, the cracking open

of their coffins, the recognition of the cost of socialism and of all past revolutions, the embrace of a utopia of revolt that arises from despair. In place of frozen history, the forgetting of history, false representations of history, the repression of truth, the perversion of language, and the substitution of violence (socialism's last argument [Müller 1989: 134]) for reason, Müller prescribes *Eingedenken*—aware action—as a way forward.

Thus in Müller's hands, the teaching play ceases to teach an ethical/political lesson within an ahistorical, closed framework. His teaching plays are exacerbations of the tension between past catastrophe and present ethical action, that is, exercises in *Eingedenken*. Once Müller's teaching plays are viewed as exercises in historical truth-telling in the name of political engagement and ethical action, they are not too difficult to adapt to American historical and ethical circumstances. I will give two brief examples of teaching plays that exemplify *Eingedenken*, with an eye toward their reception by an American audience, in particular students.

The most straightforward case is Müller's short 1968 play *The Horatian*, loosely based on a teaching play by Brecht. The play's conflict concerns the two equally necessary ways of judging a soldier who, as champion of the Roman side, first vanquishes and kills the enemy champion in single combat, and then kills his own sister when she expresses grief at the killing of this man, whom she was to marry. This situation is easily read as an allegory of the contradiction between Stalin's service to humanity as the principal vanquisher of Hitler and his culpability as a murderer rivaling or surpassing Hitler. The Soviet bloc's response to the contradiction had been to dissemble and temporize, despite Khrushchev's 1956 secret speech to the Soviet 20th Party Congress, or indeed because of its secrecy, which sent a clear signal that the disavowal of Stalinism did not mean the dismantling of the repressive Stalinist system. Müller, in contrast, follows his characteristic strategy of heightening rather than minimizing the dialectic offered him by history. The judgment on the Horatian is both to honor him as the savior of Rome, and to execute him as the murderer of his sister. And in an act of *Eingedenken*, neither of these judgments is to be spoken without equal acknowledgement of the other:

And one of the Romans asked the others:
What shall we call the Horatian for those after us?
And the people answered with one voice:
He shall be called the conqueror of Alba
He shall be called the murderer of his sister
Within one breath his merit and his guilt.
And whoever speaks of his guilt and not of his merit

Shall dwell where the dogs dwell, as a dog
And whoever speaks of his merit and not of his guilt
He, too, shall dwell among dogs.
But he who speaks of his guilt at one time
And at other times speaks of his merit
Differently speaking with one mouth at different times
Or differently to different ears
His tongue shall be torn from his mouth.
Since the words must be kept pure.
(Müller 1990: 115)

Even though the drama evokes Stalin and the half-hearted attempt by Khrushchev to exorcise his ghost, the universality of mendacious political speech is so evident as to scarcely need comment. But this familiar state of affairs may also facilitate a confrontation with Müller's uncompromising embrace of contradiction, of a generative dialectic that can motivate ethical action rather than a univocal narrative bent on closure, avoidance of visible conflict, and the sale of wars or products.

The classroom is one of the few venues available for demonstrating what dialectical thought looks like, and offering practice in its application. Despite the rise of alternative news media (mailing lists, online news magazines, blogs, wikis), mass media in the firmly 20th Century sense continue to shape 21st Century American opinion by regurgitating government press releases and reporting on governmentally-staged news events. The alternative media themselves, with their narrow audiences and predilection to raucous polemic instead of careful fact-checking, offer few examples of the analytical clarity needed to counter a well-oiled propaganda machine. Students arrive in college unable to negotiate contradictory assessments of the world and unwilling to subject their own assumptions to critical analysis, and are thus the perfect audience and actors for a neo-Brechtian teaching play that forces them to hold incommensurable ideas in play instead of rushing to facile resolution. The collapse of public confidence in the U.S. administration's foreign adventurism and domestic surveillance offers an ideal moment to reflect on the dialectic of past errors and present obligations – our own and others'. Teaching plays such as *The Horation* impose a rigor of thought that transcends their apparent dramatic crudeness and affords their exotic plots a degree of moral urgency that can startle Americans much as they did East Germans. Occupying the historically aware subject positions laid out by Müller in his plays is a subversive act in any political milieu.

The second instructive case is the 1970 play *Mauser*, a dramatization of necessary killing during the Russian Civil War of 1917-1922, a struggle between the Bolsheviks and the pro-monarchist, anti-Communist White forces. The play is also an analysis of the damage done to socialism by the ensuing Stalinist savagery, which Müller sees as a fanatical rapture of destruction completely opposite to Marxist class-consciousness.

In 1988 Hörnigk turned to me in the midst of discussing this play and asked me to apply it to America: What equivalent could I find to the necessity of killing enemies in the name of the revolution? The question baffled me, but I would remember it many years later as I brought *Mauser* and other Müller texts to American students who, having come of age after the Cold War ended, had no clear idea even of what Communism was, let alone knowledge of the particulars of the Russian Civil War. What analogy was there to draw between, on the one hand, Müller's assertion that "the daily bread of the Revolution / In the city of Witebsk as in other cities / Is the death of its enemies" (Müller 1990: 121-122), and, on the other hand, the mediated, consumerist "ecstasy, numbness, oblivion" of postmodern America?

The answer lies once more in the play's illustration of *Eingedenken*. Müller based *Mauser* on Brecht's *The Measures Taken* and begins where Brecht leaves off, presenting a character ("B") who, like the Young Comrade of the earlier play, is unable to suppress his emotional impulses and submit to Party discipline. This, however, is merely prologue to the main business of the play, which is the quite different failure exhibited by the protagonist "A." After carrying out the death sentence on B, who had taken pity on three condemned men and freed them, A takes over B's task of eliminating the enemies of the revolution. Soon he experiences the same doubts as B, recognizing himself in the working people he is assigned to kill. Unable to resolve the contradiction, his consciousness begins to split in two (Marxist alienation par excellence), a motif echoed structurally throughout the play and in the stage directions:

> And my revolver aimed at his neck now
> I wheel gallows rope garrote knout katorga
> I before my revolver aimed at my neck.
> Knowing, with my hand the Revolution kills
> Abolishing wheel gallows rope garrote knout katorga
> And not knowing it, before my revolver a man
> I between hand and revolver, finger and trigger
> I breach in my consciousness, in our front.
> (Müller 1990: 128)

This breach in consciousness (in the *Bewusstsein* spoken of in the *Manifesto of the Communist Party* [Section II], the social or class consciousness which emerges from crises of survival) is both personal and political, an inability to unite thought and action, and it opens a breach not just in his consciousness but also in the front of revolutionary battle. However, unlike B, A listens to the instructions of the Chorus, which justifies the killing by problematizing the notion of Man itself:

> Your mandate is not to kill men but
> Enemies. Namely, Man is unknown.
> Not until the Revolution has finally triumphed . . .
> Will we know what that is, Man.
> (Müller 1990: 128)

However, A absorbs the wrong lesson from this facile Marxist chestnut, and the gap between action and thought widens into madness:

> I have thrown off my burden
> On my neck the dead don't trouble me any longer
> A man is something you shoot into
> Until Man will rise from the ruins of man. . . .
> I take under my boot what I have killed
> I dance on my dead with stomping steps
> For me it isn't enough to kill what must die
> So the Revolution will triumph and the killing end
> But it shouldn't be here any more and be nothing forever
> And disappear from the face of the earth
> A clean slate for those who will come.
> (Müller 1990: 129)

The implications of A's new attitude are clear from the foregoing discussion. Rather than acknowledging the cost of the Revolution, assisting the historical dead in cracking open their coffins and joining a historical movement that remains open, A seeks to annihilate history and to start over with a "clean slate," beginning with the murder of his own consciousness, and ending in a war crime. The burden of mindfulness must not be thrown off. The opposite of *Eingedenken* turns out to be insanity and the betrayal of everything the Revolution stands for, the exchange of lucid action for exuberant murder and a succinct allegory of Stalinist bloodlust. The chorus regards A with horror:

> We heard his roaring and saw what he had done
> Not by our mandate, and he didn't stop screaming
> With the voice of Man who is devouring Man.
> Then we knew that his work had used him up . . . .
> (Müller 1990: 129)

In order to further the Revolution, A must now die. His crime: Ceasing to be an ethical agent in history, succumbing to "the sleep of machines" (Müller 1990: 130). A ultimately consents to his sentence as Brecht's Young Comrade had consented to his.

In a classroom or workshop setting, *Mauser* offers a subtle and far-reaching critique of students' received ideas and ideological commitments, not just by forcing attention to the dialectic of history (as in *The Horatian*), but by relocating that dialectic inside the consciousness of a historical agent. By depicting a man's descent into madness under the pressure of history, *Mauser* both personalizes the obligation of remembrance, and presents that obligation as an everyday revolutionary crisis.

The most obvious application of *Mauser* to the American experience is the acknowledgement of the nation's war crimes, whether in World War II terror bombings or in Mi Lai. These are, however, distant crimes that few students in comfortable civilian circumstances believe they have the potential to commit. Of greater interest may be the applicability of the concept of *Eingedenken* in the post-9/11 moment. How much of one's understanding of history and ethical responsibility must be jettisoned to make palatable the bugging of domestic telephone communications, the imprisonment of U.S. citizens without trial, the distortion of intelligence data to justify a war, the use of subpoenas to determine one's taste in books, the vilification of dissenters and of lawyers defending the accused, the use of "waterboarding" in secret CIA prisons, and the deportation of suspects to nations that practice torture openly? These are behaviors which fly in the face of law and morality, yet they are supposedly necessitated by a state of crisis. *Mauser* provides a template for critically examining the roots and consequences of such thinking.

Now my answer to Frank Hörnigk comes easily if I restate the question slightly: When have Americans acting on the stage of history lapsed, like Müller's A, from ethical action into mindless brutality justified by misunderstood ideals? When has patriotism turned to grinning barbarism? The photographs from Abu Ghraib are explained better by the psychology of forgetting in *Mauser* than in a thousand hand-wringing media commentaries. What if the setting of *Mauser* were shifted from Witebsk to Guantanamo? At this historical distance, disappointed belief in American exceptionalism seems not altogether different from East German authors' skeptical inquiries about the New Socialist Man. A successful teaching play, as reconfigured by Müller, is a trap that ensnares the ideological world view of its actors and audience in the dialectic of history. The intense ahistoricism of the present American moment offers a ripe and

vulnerable target for the spectacular public and private cataclysms of
Müller's drama.

Notes

[1] For this very reason, Brecht's theater became the object of suspicion and frequent
censorship at the hands of East German authorities. For a study of Brecht's
struggles against the strange brew of philistinism and Stalinist political orthodoxy
in the culture ministry, see Joachim Lucchesi's book *Das Verhör in der Oper*, a
documentation of the government effort to suppress the early 1950s Brecht/Dessau
opera *The Condemnation of Lucullus*.

[2] "Morality, religion, metaphysics, all the rest of ideology and their corresponding
forms of consciousness, thus no longer retain the semblance of independence.
They have no history, no development...." (Marx and Engels, *The German
Ideology*: I, A, 4). Ideology has no history because it is merely an effect of material
reality, not reality itself.

[3] All translations from the German are my own except for Carl Weber's renderings
of Heiner Müller's plays *Hamletmachine*, *The Horation*, *Mauser*, and *The Task*.

[4] The seminal 1925 novel *Cement* by Fyodor Gladkov (1883-1958), which would
later serve as the basis for a Müller play of the same name, displays many of the
characteristics that would be codified in the 1930s as Socialist Realism: resolute,
near-superhuman heroes, contemptible counter-revolutionaries, the growth of class
consciousness through political action and ideological struggle, and the ultimate
defeat of careerist bureaucrats. While offering sometimes far-fetched glimpses of
the New Socialist Man, the novel is remarkable for dramatizing the human cost of
socialist progress and depicting the sectarian divisions that characterized the
relatively free-wheeling Leninist period of the Soviet Union. The considerably
more fervid 1936 novel *How the Steel was Tempered* by Nikolai Ostrovsky (1904-
1936) became a cornerstone of the Socialist Realist canon with its depiction of the
iconic Pavel Korchagin, who overcomes multiple disabilities to serve the socialist
cause.   See my overview elsewhere (Robinson: 4-7, 27) of the substance and
duration of Socialist Realism in its East German manifestation.

[5] The term *Ankunftsliteratur* derives from Brigitte Reimann's 1961 novel *Ankunft
im Alltag* (*Arrival in the Everyday*). The canonical account (from a GDR
perspective) of this phase of literary and social development is contained in Haase
et al, 227-234 (the impulses from the Party and Writers' Union, the period of the
Bitterfelder Weg, etc.) and 523-549 (the new generation of prose writers—Christa
Wolf, Hermann Kant, and Erwin Strittmatter, among others—realistically
depicting personal development in a socialist milieu).

[6] From the ninth of the "Theses on the Philosophy of History: "A Klee painting
named 'Angelus Novus' shows an angel looking as though he is about to move
away from something he is fixedly contemplating. His eyes are staring, his mouth
is open, his wings are spread. This is how one pictures the angel of history. His
face is turned toward the past. Where we perceive a chain of events, he sees one
single catastrophe which keeps piling wreckage upon wreckage and hurls it in front

of his feet. The angel would like to stay, awaken the dead, and make whole what
has been smashed. But a storm is blowing from Paradise; it has got caught in his
wings with such violence that the angel can no longer close them. This storm
irresistibly propels him into the future to which his back is turned, while the pile of
debris before him grows skyward. This storm is what we call progress" (Benjamin,
Illuminations: 259-261).

Work Cited

Benjamin, Walter (1968). *Illuminations.* Ed. Hannah Arendt. Trans. Harry
Zohn. New York: Harcourt, Brace & World.

—. *Der Passagen-Werk, Vol. 1 (*1982). Ed. Rolf Tiedemann. Frankfurt am
Main: Suhrkamp.

Brecht, Bertolt (2000). "The Measures Taken. Lehrstück." Trans. Carl R.
Mueller. *The Measures Taken and other Lehrstücke.* Eds. John Willett
and Ralph Mannheim. New York: Arcade: 7-34.

Gladkov, Fyodor Vasilievich (1980). *Cement.* Trans. A.S. Arthur and C.
Ashleigh. New York: Continuum.

Haase, Horst et al (1977). *Literatur der Deutschen Demokratischen
Republik. [Geschichte der deutschen Literatur.* Band 11.] Berlin:
Volk und Wissen.

Hörnigk, Frank (1990). *"Texte, die auf Geschichte warten...:* Zum
Geschichtsbegriff bei Heiner Müller." *Heiner Müller Material: Texte
und Kommentare.* Leipzig: Reclam: 123-137.

Lucchesi, Joachim, ed (1993). *Das Verhör in der Oper: Die Debatte um
Brecht/Dessaus "Lukullus" 1951.* Berlin: BasisDruck.

Marx, Karl and Friedrich Engels.*The German Ideology.* Marxists Internet
Achive. 12 January 2007.
<http://www.marxists.org/archive/marx/works/1845/german-
ideology/ch01a.htm#p27>.

—. *Manifesto of the Communist Party. Marxists Internet Achive. 12
January 2007.*
<http://www.marxists.org/archive/marx/works/1848/communist-
manifesto/index.htm>.

Müller, Heiner (1978). "Verabschiedung des Lehrstücks." Letter to Reiner
Steinweg (4 January 1977). *Mauser.* Berlin: Rotbuch: 85.

—. (1984). *Hamletmachine and Other Texts for the Stage.* Ed and trans.
Carl Weber. New York: Performing Arts Journal Publications.
[Contains *Hamletmachine* and *The Task.*]

—. (1989). *Explosion of a Memory: Writings of Heiner Müller.* Ed. and
trans. Carl Weber. New York: PAJ Publications. [Contains
Volokolamsk Highway III: The Duel.]

—. (1990). *The Battle: Plays, Poetry, Prose by Heiner Müller*. Ed. and trans. Carl Weber. New York: Performing Arts Journal Publications. [Contains *The Horation* and *Mauser.*]

—. (1998). "Der glücklose Engel." *Die Gedichte*. Ed. Frank Hörnigk. Frankfurt am Main: Suhrkamp: 53.

Robinson, David W (1999). *Deconstructing East Germany: Christoph Hein's Literature of Dissent*. Rochester, NY: Camden House.

Zhdanov, A. A. "Soviet Literature—The Richest in Ideas, the Most Advanced Literature." Address to the Soviet Writers Congress, 1934. Marxists Internet Archive. 15 May 2005. http://www.marxists.org/subject/art/lit_crit/sovietwritercongress/zdhanov.htm.

CHAPTER EIGHT

AFTER IDEOLOGY:
HEINER MÜLLER AND THE THEATRE
OF CATASTROPHE

DAVID KILPATRICK

Despite his efforts to "consistently avoid identification" (Müller 1990: 191), Heiner Müller is often understood as a "Marxist playwright," his works seen in a continuum going back to Brecht as a response to Marx. Such an approach emphasizes the ideological aspects of his drama and his personal commitment to the utopian project of the German Democratic Republic (GDR). But Müller's dramaturgy developed, from the 1970s on, into a poetic medium that resists the conventions of linear plot and character development in such a way that a coherent theme/ideology is not just elusive but impossible. In interviews, Müller often claims that ideology is simply used as material in his plays, and that he is more interested in being carried along with language. This suggests that his position as dramatist is outside of ideology or—perhaps most accurately— after the time in which ideology matters. Even if we are to read Müller's plays in the context of the GDR, we must nonetheless do so after the collapse of the Berlin Wall, in the wake of the death of its utopian project.

This is to push Müller studies in the direction of a continuum going back to Artaud as a response to Nietzsche. His unique form of a theatre of cruelty allows for language to sweep aside the subjective positions of characters, and instead stage meditations on the catastrophic loss of fixed positions, from self and ideology to God. Müller's is a post-ideological, post-theological drama, written for a theatre of catastrophe in which radical uncertainty violates any possibility of belief or opinion, much less truth. The parallels to the theory of contemporary British dramatist, Howard Barker, whose "theatre of catastrophe" likewise charts out a dramaturgy of radical uncertainty, will be emphasized. Müller claimed that Artaud's works would one day be "read on the ruins of Europe" and be recognized as "classics" (Müller 1990: 175). The time has come for Müller's plays to be read on these ruins, and if they are to be recognized as classics, they must be approached from a post-ideological perspective. In this spirit, I will conclude with a brief treatment of *Hamletmaschine* and *Bildbeschreibung* [*Explosion of a Memory/ Description of a Picture*] as examples of catastrophic dramaturgy.

In an interview with André Müller the playwright claims, "I'm no ideologue. I use Marxism as material, in the same way I use a Shakespeare play or a ride on the trolley. This becomes form and is valid as such. I am only interested in my writing" (Müller 1990: 202). This is antithetical to the dramaturgy of Brecht, which places itself in the service of ideology. Indeed, Brecht insists that, "the epic theatre is a moral institution" (Brecht: 75). This moralizing or didactic element is at the heart of epic theatre, the *Verfremdungseffekt* a means of resisting empathy or escapism.

There is no question that Müller's plays feature a form of alienation. But his is a *Verfremdungseffekt* in which no learning is possible, as he complicates the viewer's subjective position vis-à-vis the staged action. In Brecht, the audience is assured a static position, as reason is reified, in order for the lesson to be learned and carried out as social action. For Brecht, writing drama, making theatre, is always (at least after his expressionist period) done with a purpose. Müller, on the other hand, in his interview with André Müller, claims that, "When I write, all I want to do is write, I am not interested in a purpose" (Müller 1990: 209) or again to Jonathan Kalb: "I have no ideology when I write" (Kalb 1993: 71). So why have so many approached his writings attempting either to determine his purpose or to serve their own ideological aims?

When placing Müller's work in the context of literary, theatrical and cultural history, or attempting to explore the influences on his dramaturgy, the single name that is mentioned first and foremost is that of Brecht. Once, Müller was asked to name an influence other than Brecht his response was, "I'm sorry, but I have few influences" (qtd. Kalb 2001: 104). The response is characteristic, typical of Müller (not to reduce him to a character or type), playfully dancing around the presumption inherent in the question. One takes the influence of Brecht as a given, and this precedence isn't challenged.

I am not claiming that Brecht was not an influence. There is no doubt that Müller learned from Brecht, and revered him as a seminal influence. But like any worthy student/son he—in Oedipal fashion—kills the teacher/father.

So I find it necessary in this context, as we explore the "cultural politics of Heiner Müller" to counter: he has none. At least with his works from *Hamletmachine* on. Given his insistence to Carl Weber that he is "neither a dope—nor a hope—dealer" (Müller 1984: 140), why invest his plays with any (politicized) hope? To do so is to resist the tragic consciousness his plays expose. His texts cannot be therapeutic, socially or personally. And so I offer this as a response to Dan Friedman, when he says in his introduction to the first volume of *Müller in America* that Müller's "texts are an ongoing deconstruction of theatrical convention, his politics Marxist" (Friedman: 18). I absolutely agree with the former, but take issue with the latter. Not to make as crude a gesture as a rejection, but rather as a complication.

The post-ideological is post-theological, its necessary consequence, as ideology is what is left of the remains of God, a final idol manifest in the transcendent ideal. The idea/l of communism is a last means of resisting the tragic night of non-knowledge, a final science, system or meta-structure by which human existence can oppose the movement of time, the truth of death. The only truth. Which is, of course, its absence. Hamlet. Ideology is a final delusion, a desperate last-gasp intervention, and Müller's plays are an awakening from this dream, this fantasy of a meaningful existence, that one's existence can be worthy of a meaning.

Artaud insists: "We are not free. And the sky can still fall on our heads. And the theater has been created to teach us that first of all" (Artaud: 79). This is the only lesson offered by a theatre of cruelty. Such a theatre is antithetical to Brechtian didacticism, for it destabilizes subjectivity and disrupts any rational knowing self who might benefit from the theatrical action. Indeed, this benefit is allied with loss and expenditure, as nothing can be gained from such a theatre.

There is, of course, nothing new in citing the Artaudian strain in Müller's texts. As Jonathan Kalb observes, "Nearly every dissertation and book-length study on Müller contains a separate section, if not an entire chapter, summarizing Artaud's theories and establishing affinities between the two writers that are then held to be fundamental" (Kalb 2001: 104-5). But Kalb goes on to insist that Müller's "relationship to Artaud was tactical" (Kalb 2001: 120). And here I think Kalb overstates the case. Müller would surely say, as he did with Brecht, that to "use [him] without criticizing him is betrayal" (Müller 1990: 133). Kalb places his argument in relation to Michael Schneider's condemnation of plays from *Hamletmachine* on as symptomatic of a psychological crisis or dysfunction. Schneider's argument is itself an updating of earlier condemnations of Müller's Marxist apostasy. Kalb tries to distance Müller from any identification with an Artaudian collapse of subjectivity. Thus his emphasis on a "tactical" appropriation of Artaud is an attempt to reify authorial integrity. Like Shakespearean criticism that insists that Hamlet is but feigning madness, Kalb's argument runs, so too Müller is simply "borrowing a complexion of authentic pathology to lure us into a diabolical literary-funhouse where he could administer his own version of cruelty" (Kalb 2001: 120). What is gained in such a rhetorical gesture? Much like those who want to dismiss any hint that Hamlet might be just a bit mad, Kalb wants us to see Müller as one who simply mimics madness, his adaptation of a theatre of cruelty not an experience, not an exploration of a tragic mode of consciousness, but an elegant theatrical conceit.

The more accurate assessment of Müller's difference from Artaud should not be found in privileging the rational integrity of one over the other, or playing the author-function in this overly psychologizing manner. Instead, it is fairer to say that if Artaud's theatre is modern, then Müller's is a postmodern theatre of cruelty, reminding us that the sky can fall on our heads, but without the synthesis or unification of a ritualized collectivity of author-actors-audience.

Müller himself did not view Artaud's collapse as weakness or flaw. Instead he notes that "The lightning that split Artaud's consciousness was Nietzsche's experience, it could be the last. The emergency is Artaud. He tore literature away from the police, theater away from medicine. Under the sun of torture, which shines equally on all the continents of this planet, his texts blossom" (Müller 1990: 175). The stakes involved for consciousness are not so easily dismissed, as if their staging was a careful calculation. There is instead an historical exigency to such a thought, this tragic thought that could be the last experience—the experience of the last. Müller's texts attend to this crisis of consciousness. To ascribe an ideological motive for his most important works is to police his writing, to make his theatre medicinal; precisely what his work from *Hamletmachine* on avoids.

So Kalb makes the mistake of seeing Müller's work in relation to Artaud in terms of theatrical technique, rather than its place at the end of the Western tradition as a mode of tragic consciousness. Kalb wants to reject the experiential aspect of this. And the link Müller makes with Artaud to Nietzsche is most instructive, as it offers an alternative heritage to that of Brecht back to Marx. It isn't that Müller's mind is either in or out of crisis (and that by taking the position that the author isn't really in crisis he can be defended against those critics who would dismiss his work), but an awareness that *thought itself is in crisis* and that the dramatist can no longer serve as cultural policeman, physician or therapist.

Kalb claims that, "Müller wants us to hear a Nietzschean echo, but only an echo" (Kalb 2001: 118). I would insist instead that he wants us to hear the thunder that accompanies the lightning that split the consciousness of Artaud, the *blitzwitz* of the Nietzschean experience. It is worth noting that Müller read Nietzsche long before he read Marx, just after the war, in his late teens (Müller 1990: 69-70). The influence precedes and ultimately exceeds that of Marx, as his theatre must be understood as action taken in the wake of the death of God, if not the staging of deicidal action. In *Writing and Difference*, Derrida uses the term "nontheological space" to describe what is produced in Artaud's theatre of cruelty (Derrida: 235). But this is best understood as post-theological space, and applies equally well to Müller's dramaturgy.

This is a uniquely contemporary mode of tragedy (we can argue the question of modern/postmodern), and Müller's exploration of an experience of tragic consciousness is emphasized with his frequent use of the term "catastrophe" to convey the subject or source of his dramatic texts. In an interview with Horst Laube he says, "The true pleasure of writing consists, after all, in the enjoyment of catastrophe" (Müller 1990: 190). When he repeats this sense of "pleasure in the catastrophe" in an interview with Kalb, the interviewer insists, "But to emphasize the catastrophe, that's madness." Recall now Kalb's rejection of madness in Müller. But the dramatist responds, "Only for nondramatists. Drama has always been concerned with catastrophe. It needs catastrophe" (Kalb 1993: 77). For Müller, theatre must not suppress or exclude the catastrophic. Instead, theatre must embrace catastrophe, recognize it as its source.

This brings to mind the theoretical writings of English dramatist Howard Barker, who calls his approach "theatre of catastrophe." Teasing out an affinity between their conceptions of tragedy should not be a reductive exercise, but must allow for each to be seen in light of a crisis that persists in the contemporary theatre. Like Müller, Barker began his career as a leftist writer, but his dramaturgy took a decidedly post-theological turn. While he sees his theatre of catastrophe as a form of theatrical cruelty, he distinguishes his own work from Artaud's project in his privileging of language. The role of language in Müller is itself an interesting question vis-à-vis Artaud, inasmuch as Müller is first and foremost a writer. But one must be cautious of confusing Artaud's project from that of his disciples, as his rejection of logocentrism (so often cited as an appeal for a theatre of images) is not truly a suppression of poetic language. Artaud himself was first and foremost a writer. So the question of the writing in the theatres of Müller, Artaud and Barker deserves further attention. But it must be stated clearly that Barker's drama emphasizes the sovereignty of language.

Barker acknowledges an indebtedness to Nietzsche, and reserves special contempt for the didacticism of Brechtian (and Shavian) theatre, and defines the unique conditions for his own form of tragedy in contrast with classical conceptions of tragic drama:

> Traditional tragedy was a restatement of public morality over the corpse of the transgressive protagonist—thus Brecht saw catharsis as essentially passive. But in a theatre of Catastrophe there is not restoration of certitudes, and in a sense more compelling and less manipulated than in the Epic theatre, it is the audience which is freed into authority. In a culture now so rampantly populist that the cultural distinctions of right and left have evaporated, the public have a right of access to a theatre that is neither brief nor relentlessly uplifting, but which insists on complexity and pain, and the beauty that can only be created from the spectacle of pain. In Catastrophe, whose imaginative ambition exposes the reactionary content in the miserabilism of everyday life, lies the possibility of reconstruction. (Baker: 54)

Such a theatre rejects the false security afforded by the bourgeois appeal to established social mores, the boredom of an existence that precludes the tragic. Barker refuses to be a hope-dealer.

This is not to suggest that Barker's plays are like Müller's. Barker does not complicate plot or character to the degree that Müller does from *Hamletmachine* on. The theoretical affinity is found in their emphases on the catastrophic, on a new form of tragedy that resists ideology or any subservience of drama to morality and message. Barker praises the "Disappointing play," for while it avoids didacticism, it likewise avoids entertainment. Instead it complicates and polemicizes, leaving the audience with questions that linger and disturb, "and instead of offering the reward, it delivers the wound," promoting a state of anxiety, which "will come from the audience's attempt to experience the play outside the confines of ideology" (Baker: 68). A form of theatrical cruelty, the audience are (not is) denied a unifying thematic principle and are instead thrown into their own individual radical uncertainties (that again further complicate any static sense of self).

To bring Barker's theatre of catastrophe into relation with Müller is not to say that their plays are of the same ilk, but to extend Barker's dramatic theory beyond its application to his own plays, and those of his disciples (such as Sarah Kane), which is as far as Barker studies have gone. I would argue that drama as disparate as that of Hermann Nitsch, Neil LaBute, or Richard Foreman would benefit from being viewed as forms of theatre of catastrophe, and that this is especially the case with Müller's texts.

We can therefore see in *Hamletmachine* (1977) a form of catastrophic theatre. In Shakespeare the social order is restored at play's end, but this is hardly the case in Müller. Ideology requires a fixed point of view, it must be on one side or other of the revolution, but the Actor Playing Hamlet says, "My place, if my drama would still happen, would be on both sides of the front, between the frontlines, over and above them. I stand in the stench of the crowd and hurl stones at policemen soldiers tanks bullet-proof glass. I look through the double doors of bullet-proof glass at the crowd pressing forward and smell the sweat of my fear" (Müller 1984: 56). His experience, his consciousness, is not restricted to those who are for or against the revolt. He is the terror; the catastrophe conjured by the revolution.

The extended monologue structure of *Hamletmachine* is an attempt to think through the tragic consciousness. Tearing the author's photograph, the Actor Playing Hamlet says, "My thoughts are lesions in my brain. My brain is a scar. I want to be a machine" (Müller 1984: 57). This is not mere mimicry of subjective crisis, a tactical adaptation, but a playing out of the death of the author as an exposure to cruelty on an ontological scale. This cannot be reclaimed by any ideological position, cannot support a political agenda.

With *Bildbeschreibung* [*Explosion of a Memory/Description of a Picture*] (1984), Müller furthers his experiment with tragic consciousness and catastrophic dramatugurgy, abandoning the character-based assignation of speech (dialogue or monologue) altogether in a stream of language that communicates the anguish that attends the collapse of the onto-theo-logical. A six-page sentence in which words spew out images, which are just as quickly disrupted in poetic movement of orgiastic violence: "the peephole into Time will open between one glimpse and the next, hope lives on the edge of the knife that rotates ever faster, with increasing attention that equals fatigue, insecurity lightening the certainty of the ultimate horror," challenging us "TO LIVE IN A MIRROR" (Müller 1989: 102). The text is not just the explosion of a memory but memory as explosion, staging (in writing) the experience of catastrophic consciousness. Although the text is about viewing, a description of a picture, the picture described refuses any fixed point-of-view. This dislocation of rational thought cannot be reinscribed within any system of thought, ideology, or significatory order. It marks the collapse of all significatory orders.

David Bathrick reminds us that "Müller always insisted that he was not a 'political' writer" and asks, "what does it mean to trace and interpret Müller's purported 'anti-Westernism' in relation to Müller's own richly tic style of writing? Must everything be read simply as philosophical or political allegory?” (Bathrick: 32). Approaching Müller’s texts as a theatre of catastrophe is not to read his works allegorically. They do not stand in for that which can be said more simply. Rather, they perform this philosophical crisis, the unraveling of Cartesian security with the death of God.

Ultimately, we can see in Müller’s work a rejection of Hegel’s sentiment that “the wounds of Spirit heal, and leave no scars behind” (Hegel 1997: §669; 407). His plays refuse the healing process of any ideology that would eliminate the scars of History and the memory of pain they signify. If Müller’s texts are to be understood politically, it is in the spirit of a Nietzschean *große Politik* (Nietzsche: §208; 321). That is, not the petty politics of competing isms, but the struggle for the future of the planet. It begins, after ideology, with thought’s exposure to and engagement with the catastrophic.

Work Cited

Artaud, Antonin (1958). *The Theater and Its Double*. Trans. Mary Caroline Richards. New York: Grove.
Barker, Howard (1997). *Arguments for a Theatre*. 3rd ed. New York: Manchester University Press.
Bathrick, David (1998). “The Provocation of his Images.” *New German Critique* 73 (Winter 1998): 31-34.
Brecht, Bretolt (1964). “Theatre for Pleasure of Theatre for Instruction.” *Brecht on Theatre*. Trans. John Willett. New York: Hill and Wang: 69-76.
Derrida, Jacques (1978). *Writing and Difference*. Trans. Alan Bass. Chicago: University of Chicago Press.
Friedman, Dan (2003). “Introduction.” *Müller in America*. Vol. 1. New York: Castillo Cultural Center.
Hegel, G.W. (1977). *The Phenomenology of Spirit*. Trans. A.V. Miller. Oxford: Oxford University Press.
Kalb, Jonathan (1993). *Free Admissions*. New York: Limelight.
—. (2001). *The Theater of Heiner Müller*. Rev. ed. New York: Limelight.
Müller, Heiner (1984). *Hamletmachine and Other Texts for the Stage*. Ed. and trans. Carl Weber. New York: Performing Arts Journal Publications.
—. (1989). *Explosion of a Memory*. Ed and trans. Carl Weber. New York: Performing Arts Journal Publications.

—. (1990). *Germania*. Ed. Sylvère Lotringer. Trans. Bernard and Caroline Schütze. New York: Semiotext(e).

Nietzsche, Friedrich (1968). *Beyond Good and Evil*. Trans. Walter Kaufmann. *Basic Writings of Nietzsche*. New York: Modern Library: 181-435.

CHAPTER NINE

BLOOMING BUZZING CONFUSION

FRED NEWMAN AND DAN FRIEDMAN

Since we are baseball fans as well as theatre directors and playwrights, perhaps it's not surprising that Heiner Müller reminds us of Casey Stengel.

Charles Dillon Stengel was a baseball player and manager who lived from 1890 to 1975. He was given the name "Casey" by his fellow ballplayers because he was from, Kansas City (K.C.). He was a fairly good baseball player, who played professionally from 1912 to 1923. He played in three World Series, with the Brooklyn Dodgers in 1916 and with the New York Giants in 1922 and 1923. However, it is as a manager that he left his mark on baseball. Some baseball fans, including us, consider Stengel the greatest manager of all time—and, as we hope to demonstrate, he was an important manager for reasons analogous to what makes Müller an important playwright.

Stengel started by managing his old team, the Dodgers, during the 1933 and 1934 seasons. He then went to the Boston Braves from 1938 to 1943. He didn't do very well with either and was forced to manage in the minor leagues for the rest of the forties. In 1949, to the surprise of many, the New York Yankees, already the nation's dominant club, decided to give him a chance at the helm. The Yankees, under his leadership, went on to win a still-unmatched five consecutive World Series (1949 to 1953) and ten pennants over the next 12 years.

However, before we consider what made Stengel a great manager, we'd like to examine how he spoke, how he used language, because we think it's connected to how he approached managing a baseball team and because both are connected, we think, to how Müller wrote plays and approached the theatre. Stengel spoke a strange language. It was English, one could recognize that, but it was such a distinct form of English that after awhile it was given a name—Stengelize. He never constricted himself to a standard subject-predicate form of talk. In the middle of sentences he would introduce new subjects, new verbs. It was hard to follow because he broke up standard syntax, but it actually gave, we think, a more accurate picture of what he was thinking about.

Lev Vygotsky, an early 20th Century Marxist psychologist, made a very radical proposition/discovery based on his observations of how children learn to speak. He maintained that language is not the *expression* of thought as much as the active *completion* of thought. This is, we think, a very helpful distinction because it dissolves the dichotomy between thought and language—the commonly held assumption that words are tools to "give expression" to thoughts that are already fully formed in our minds. Instead, Vygotsky posits that thought and language are a unity, that language is not simply the material, social expression of thought, it is the completion of the thought process. Thus thought itself is understood not as an abstraction "in your head," but as a social activity. What Vygotsky creates is a different and new ontological unit that gets beyond the mind/body distinction of Western tradition (Vygotsky).

What Vygotsky didn't deal with (and this is not a criticism, after all, he was a psychologist, not a philosopher or an artist) is that there are various ways of completing. Traditional language has the failing of making it seem as if the only thing that's going on is the thing you are identifying in the particular linear sentence that you're uttering. It was the philosopher Ludwig Wittgenstein who helped us grapple with the endless ways in which thought might be completed by language. Although he didn't use the term "completing," he was fascinated by the contradictory nature of language—that it can simultaneously function as a prison that locks up our imagination and that it can be played with, shaped, transformed in ways that liberate our imagination. Wittgenstein's core insight, as far as we're concerned, is that human beings get very hobbled by the traditional ways that they use language and have a hard time recognizing that it has an infinitude of uses (Wittgenstein). That's why poets like Casey Stengel and Heiner Müller come in handy—they are constantly playing/experimenting with language, seeking out ways to break free of or expand or transform our traditional ways of speaking/writing, and thus, if we accept Vygotsky's premise that thought and language are a unity, freeing or expanding or transforming the very ways we think.

Yogi Berra, something of a player-with-language himself, who was catcher for the Yankees during the great dynasty that Stengel led, said of his manager, "He could fool you. When Casey wanted to make sense, he could. But he usually preferred to make you laugh" (Berra). Certainly, Stengel enjoyed being funny. As a player, he would sometimes put a sparrow under his cap. When the crowd would applaud him for making a good play, he would doff his cap and the bird would fly out much to the delight of the fans. But with all due respect, we think Berra is missing the bigger point. Stengel chose not to make sense because making sense meant keeping himself locked inside the box. It meant confining himself to traditional ways of thinking, and consciously or otherwise, he knew that making sense could lead to nothing new. What is "sense," after all, but an agreed upon set of assumptions about thinking passed down from generation to generation? Like the Talking Heads, we firmly believe that if we human beings are going to progress at this point in history, we have to find ways to "Stop Making Sense."

Which brings us around to Stengel's way of managing and how it was connected to his way of speaking. Before Stengel started managing the Yankees, a baseball game was played (with exception of an injury or a failing pitcher) with the same nine players, presumably the team's best—this despite the fact that a team is allowed to have 22 players in its employ at any given time. This made so much "sense," that it was assumed to be the only way you could play the game. Stengel started experimenting with something new: he began moving players in and out of the game based on who he thought could do the best job in a particular situation. If a batter had a bad record against the pitcher on the mound, Stengel replaced him with a batter who would probably do better against that pitcher. If a pitcher had trouble with left-handed hitters and a lefty was coming to the plate, Stengel would replace him with a pitcher who had a better record against left-handers. He moved players who could hit the best into the line-up for the early innings and then benched them for better fielders later in the game, after the team had established a lead. In short, he started doing with players on the field what he did with nouns and verbs in a sentence. Don Larson, who pitched for Stengel's Yankees (and who, in 1956, pitched the only perfect game in World Series history) said of Stengel, "He made what some people called stupid moves, but about eight or nine out of ten of them worked" (Larson).

In retrospect, the "stupid moves" were only stupid in terms of what "made sense" in baseball logic that proceeded him. As Larson says, his stupid moves worked. The Yankees won five consecutive World Series, often against teams that were "better" than them according to the previous assumptions and traditions of baseball. Stengel changed what it means to be a good team. His method came to be called platooning and today everyone does it. It's how baseball is played.

We think that what Müller was attempting to with theatre is very similar to what Stengel was attempting with baseball. He wants it to stop making sense—not in the simplistic sense of its content being nonsensical or absurd; that's nothing new. His challenge, we believe, is more profound because it questions the very grammar of doing theatre, much as Stengel challenged the grammar of playing baseball. Müller, like Stengel, speaks a strange language. It is theatre, one can recognize that, but, from *Cement* (1974) on, he so mangles the standard syntax of theatre, that it is hardly recognizable as such. Many theatre audiences and many theatre artists—and we include ourselves among them—when they first encounter Müller find his work utterly incomprehensible. We find that exciting and encouraging. We all find "Law and Order" comprehensible. We find *The Lion King* and *Les Miserables* comprehensible. We find *Angels in America, The Coast of Utopia* and *The Vertical Hour* comprehensible. To have what we know—or think we know—reinforced is comforting. For Müller, as for Artaud, comfort leads to stagnation. He strove to make us uncomfortable, not simply through the content of his texts (which are often quite discomforting), but more fundamentally through his subversion of the foundations of theatre's grammar. As Müller put it, "Only when a text cannot be done in theatre as it is now can it be productive for the theatre, or interesting" (Müller, 1975: 120). For us, and we like to think for Müller, this is more than an aesthetic statement. It is a political statement, a declaration of war, so to speak, against the traditional (conservatizing) role of theatre in society and a challenge to theatre artists and audiences to create something more developmental to do with performance on stage.

Müller's first important break with the grammar of theatre is the abandonment/rejection of narrative in his later work. It can, and often has been, argued that historically what differentiated theatre from the ritualized performance of tribal societies from which it appears to have evolved (and, for that matter, what differentiates theatre today from, for example, modern dance) is the story. In Western theatre from Aristotle on, plot has been essential to what theatre *is*. Plot is also essential to the traditional theatres of the East. While the structure of plot has varied widely through history and across cultures, theatre, at least until very recently, has told stories, has enacted social conflict on stage in the form of narrative.

The assumption here is that narrative is a reflection of life. In Aristotle's words, "Tragedy is an imitation of an action" (Aristotle: 7-8). Theatre is thus thought to represent or signify life just as language is, according to the common understanding, supposed to represent or signify thought. The problem with this, for us, and we think for Müller, is that narrative is not life; it is a construction we create/impose that gives a coherency to life that just isn't there. In that sense, it is a falsification of experience, a falsification that represents/contains/restricts life-as-lived within a preconstructed framework, the framework of story. That narrative, that falsification, may be very artful, very beautiful and very comforting, but what is lost is the indeterminacy of life. We sit in the theater watching a play or a movie and we wind up concerned about—and the playwright is trained to help us do this—what comes next? That's exactly what's interestingly absent in life. What comes next is simply what comes next.

Just as Wittgenstein pointed out that language can (and often does) become fossilized and hence restrict the development of thought, so artistic representation can (in this case in the form of narrative, which over the millennia has come to virtually define what drama is) over-determine what we are able to experience. Müller, when speaking of his differences with Brecht said that his task was, "not to introduce one thing after the other, which was still the law for Brecht. Now you have to bring in as many factors as possible at the same time so people are forced to make choices. That is, maybe they can't choose anymore, but they have to decide what they can assimilate first" (Brenner: 95).

In bringing in "as many factors as possible at the same time," Müller is able to offer on stage an experience of the historical that is impossible in a play constrained by the boundaries of individual characters caught up in a plot. It should be noted here, that history in Müller's work is not *past*, as in a traditional history play; history for him is an active force, very much with us all the time. Nor is history, for Müller, an abstraction outside of or other than the lives of human beings. He approaches history as species-life, human beings struggling to do something with what has been created (and destroyed) by the human beings who came before. In Müller's later plays, the whole world—past and present—is taking place on stage. The character of Frederick II is falling on his rump in the *Brandenburg Concerto 1*, so is Bismarck and Hitler. The Actor Playing Hamlet in *Hamletmachine* is also all impotent Western intellectuals and desperately compromised would-be-revolutionaries who have agonized on the stage of world history over the last four hundred years. The story (if it is there at all) doesn't over-determine the experience. The audience member is given, to borrow from William James' description of an infant's perception, a "blooming buzzing confusion" (James) on stage, which s/he can relate to unmediated by the preconceived assumptions of narrative structure. Not only do Müller's later plays have no resolution, they don't tell you, in the course of their expression, where they're going.

Müller's liberation of the stage from narrative corresponds, we think, to Müller's own painful liberation from the constraints of ideology. Rejecting ideology, we need to add, is not, as far as we're concerned, the same as not having a politic. As far as we can tell from his writings and interviews, Müller remained politically engaged to the end, committed to the struggles of the world's poor and convinced that some sort of revolutionary transformation was necessary for human progress. As he put it in 1991, "For the moment everyone seems to agree that communism has failed, but one could also say that communism has thrown off its political-ideological costume and appears naked before our eyes in the shape of immigrants. The problem remains: poverty vs. wealth" (Linzer: 12).

At the same time, his texts, at least from *Hamletmachine* forward, clearly reflect a struggle with and a disengagement from Marxism as an ideology, that is, as a closed system of knowing. By knowing, we mean the cognitively based certitude with which people have determined what is real and what is not, what is true and what is false, etc. (Newman and Holzman). In the West, at least since the Renaissance, knowing has often justified itself by comparing its conclusions to those of science, the method developed to study the natural world. In fact, knowing—and the systems of knowing that we call ideologies—have often been nothing more (and, indeed, need not be more) than the acceptance of a particular social narrative. Narrative—be it small as in a play, or mega, as in the Marxist theory of history—reinforces knowing; it is itself a form of knowing which fits experience into a cognitive formula. For Müller, ideology and narrative were thus joined at the hip and he came to the view that neither was what he, nor the theatre, could, or should, any longer be about. As early as 1984, Carl Weber quotes Müller as saying that the value of drama today is not so much the transmission of knowledge, but its ability "to make experience possible" (Weber: 28). In leaving narrative, knowing and ideology behind, Müller empowers us, as theatre artists and audience members, to shift our attention away from what he has to say to what he gives us to create with.

Müller's second fundamental challenge to the grammar of the theatre is his move, in his later work, to leave individuated character behind. Getting rid of character is also, we think, for Müller concurrent with getting rid of ideology. The contemporary concept of the individual, the self, is so widely accepted that it is difficult to for many of us to understand it as an ideological construct. Yet it is a relatively new notion in human history and hardly culturally universal. The construct of the individual emerged during the Renaissance. It is a powerful concept, clearly connected to the development of capitalism. It transformed the *entirety* of western thought, the grand narrative that is Western, and comes to be the fullest expression of it. While there was tremendous social value in the creation of the individual as the basic existential unit, there are also epistemological limitations to it, limitations that the postmodernists maintain we are running up against now. Müller, by disengaging from the assumption of individual character, opens of new possibilities for the theatre, just as Stengel's disengaging from the assumption that you always played the same nine players opened up new possibilities for baseball.

At the dramaturgical level, characters and narrative are interwoven. Characters are in a play, on the most basic level, to enable the narrative, to act out the story. Once narrative is abandoned, characters are no longer necessary, although they may remain possible. (There are plays, after all, which have little or no plot but plenty of character interaction.) Müller, however, in much of his later work, rejects both narrative and character. By playing with the integrity of these bedrocks of theatre syntax, Müller allows himself (and us) to focus on the historicality, the collectivity and the dynamics of relations rather than on the individual as the expression either of psychology or ideological position—"This is who I am." "This is what I believe." In *Hamletmachine*, for example, Electra is Ophelia is Ulrike Meinhof is the woman sitting next to you in the auditorium. What's interesting is their overlay, their relationship, how they reflect upon and transform each other, not their individual psychologies.

In an interview with Sylvère Lotringer, Müller said, "*Hamletemachine* is a choral text, a collective experience, not a personal experience. When I write 'Chorus/Hamlet,' people don't read it, they don't want to. In the West they're afraid of collective experiences, they always individualize things. But in *Hamletmachine* there are lots of Hamlets." (Müller, 1990: 75). If, as Harold Bloom has argued, Shakespeare is the playwright who first brought the individuated, psychologically distinct character to the stage (Bloom), then Müller may well turn out to be the playwright who gives the individuated character his exit line.

When theatre gives up the restraints of narrative and character, it's come a long way toward ceasing to be theatre as we have known it for two and a half millennia. What Müller's work raises, we think, is the possibility of theatre giving up its magic. Finding ways for theatre to give up its magic is, from our perspective, the core of Müller's cultural politic. (Of course, Müller is not the only one contributing to the process of challenging theatre's foundations. The work of Richard Foreman, Caryl Churchill, Anne Bogart and Tina Landau, the Wooster Group and Mabou Mines, among many others, come to mind. Here, however, our focus is on Müller's specific contributions.)

One of us (Newman) has been a therapist for forty years, and both of us have been theatre directors for decades, and we think of the "magic" of theatre much as we think of the "magic" of psychoanalysis. It's the self-conscious attempt on the part of theatre artists to make it seem as if theatre were capturing some essence of life, something deeper than you can see/feel/understand in daily life. It says, "Here's what's *really* going on," just as psychotherapy, in most of its traditions, claims a special insight into what's *really* going on with the patient's emotionality. In both cases, we consider this magic to be a falsification and a manipulation that leaves the audience or the patient less powerful and less equipped to grow.

In considering the magic of the theatre, it is helpful to pause and remind ourselves of the performatory magic that preceded it—the mimic ritual of tribal society. Tribal performance, often performed by the whole village, or by a sub-unit entrusted with a particular task, concerned itself primarily with the forces of nature. George Thomson describes it as:

> ...a magical rehearsal, in which, by mimicking in anticipation the successful operation of [for example] the quest for food, the clansmen evoked in themselves the collective and concerted energy requisite for the real task. Primitive magic is founded on the notion that, by creating the illusion that you control reality, you can actually control it. It is an illusionary technique complementary to the deficiencies of the real technique. (Thomson: 13)

As societies grew more complex, more productive and more populous, dividing into classes and castes and becoming city-centered, ritual performance enacted by the entire community to control the forces/spirits of nature gave way to what we now call theatre. Collective ritual faded and the performance ritual that replaced it, theatre, was no longer enacted by the entire social unit; the performers separated from what we now call the audience (related, perhaps, to the unified tribe giving way to class-differentiated civilization) and social conflict, not conflict with nature, became the content of the performance.

The magic, however, did not go away; it just changed. The need to control nature was superceded by the need to control the conflicts unleashed by an internally conflicted society, and a new "illusory technique complementary to the deficiencies of the real technique" was developed. The performers, instead of embodying animist spirits or gods, increasingly performed other human beings, and thus the magic became less obvious, although, we would argue, no less powerful. What the theatre has said to its audiences, in a variety of ways, since its inception is: "Here, on this stage, through the medium of our performance, we will show what is *really* going on, what the meaning(s) of your struggles *really* are. We can pull back the curtain and show you the essence behind what looks like daily life." That that "essence" so often justified or rationalized the status quo is, of course, no surprise; the whole point of the magic is to control the uncontrollable contradictions of a conflicted society.

Brecht also spoke of eliminating magic in the theatre, but the magic he was talking about was of a different, far more limited, type. Brecht disliked the magic of theatrical illusion, the pretences of realism and the mythical "suspension of disbelief." The fight against that small-time magic was won long ago. In terms of the big-time magic we're talking about, Brecht was as much a magician as the rest of them. He was still dealing with essences. What he was saying, in effect, was, "The bourgeois theatre, the Aristotelian theatre, has got the magic wrong. It doesn't reveal the *real* essence of what life is about. My theatre, Epic Theatre, thanks to me and Marx, has now got it right. I know the *real* essence." Brecht was still the great knower, a progressive knower, a Marxist knower, but a knower none-the-less. Müller's great break with Brecht, with modernism, and indeed, with 2,500 years of theatre tradition, is that he gave up trying to use the stage to provide us with knowing, with truth, with the supposed essences behind everyday life.

Müller's texts, like all theatre from Aeschylus forward, still deals with social conflict. What he has given up—by abandoning narrative and character, the two basic components of drama—is the magic. In Müller's later works nothing is being forced into a system of knowing. There are no essences, no implied, invisible assumptions about how life is structured and about who we are who live it.

As the broad range of essays in this collection make clear, there are many ways to understand Müller's cultural politic. To us as a political playwrights and directors and, above all, as long-time political organizers, what is most exciting about Müller's cultural politic, as embodied in his texts, is his struggle to liberate himself from ideology—not only from the ideology that passed for Marxism in the 20th Century, but from the ideology of the theatre, the magic that has for so long worked to control the unruly demons of civilization. Instead, what Müller gives us is beautiful and unsettling poetry that, brought to the stage, can provide us with experiences free of the essences assumed by narrative and character. That is, Müller provides us not simply with new experiences, but with a new *kind* of experience. And that, among other things, makes the experience, at least initially, incomprehensible. Müller offers no predefined meanings, no essences; he says to theatre artists and audiences, "Come play with me."

Müller, in our estimation, is offering us a whole new way to create and experience performance on stage. Whether his innovations will have the same impact on theatre that Casey Stengel's had on baseball remains to be seen. But as fans of both of them, we are rooting for him.

Work Cited

Aristotle (2004), *Poetics*. Trans. E. Lobel. White Horse, Montana: Kessinger Publishing.

Berra, Yogi. www.caseystengel.com/quotes.htm

Bloom, Harold (1998). *Shakespeare: The Invention of the Human*. New York: Riverhead Hardcover.

Brenner, Eva (1994). *"HAMLETMACHINE Onstage: A Critical Analysis of Heiner Müller's Play in Production."* DAI, New York University.

James, William (1983). *The Principles of Psychology*. Cambridge, Mass.: Harvard University Press.

Larson, Don. www.caseystengel.com/quotes_about.tm

Linzer, Martin (1991). "… ruckwarts in die Gegebwart." Zu Heiner Müller's *Mauser* Porjekt am Deutschen Theater. Gespracech mit Heiner Müller. *Theater de Zeit*. November Sonderheft. Trans. Eva Brenner: 14.

Müller, Heiner (1975). "Der Dramatiker und die Geschichte seiner Zeit. Ein Gesparach zwischen Horst Laube und Heiner Müller." *Theater Heute*, Sonderhelft. 1975: 119-207. Trans. Brenner: 76.

—. *Germania*. (1990) Ed. Sylvère Lotringer. Trans. Bernard and Caroline Schütze. New York: Semiotext(e).

Newman, Fred and Holzman, Lois (1997). *The End of Knowing: A New Developmental Way of Learning*. London: Routledge.

Thomson, George (1941). *Aeschlus and Athens: A Study in the Social Origins of Drama*. London: Lawrence & Wishart.

Vygotsky, L.S. (1987). *The Collected Works of L.S. Vygotsky, Vol. 1*. New York: Plenum.

Weber, Carl (1984). "The Pressure of Experience." *Hamletmachine and Other Texts for the Stage*. Ed. and trans. Carl Weber. New York: Performing Arts Journal Publications.

Wittgenstein, Ludwig (1958). *Philosophical Investigations*. Trans. G.E.M. Anscombe. New York: MacMillian Publishing Co., Inc.

CONTRIBUTORS

Roger Bechtel is the Director of Graduate Studies in the Department of Theatre at Miami University, Ohio. He received his Ph.D. in Dramatic and Performance Theory and Criticism from Cornell University, and also holds an M.F.A. in Acting from the Yale School of Drama and a J.D. from the New York University School of Law. Active as both a scholar and an artist, he is the author of the recently published *Past Performance: American Theatre and the Historical Imagination*, and serves as artistic director of Big Picture Group, a multimedia performance collective based in Chicago.

Eva Brenner is the founder and artistic director of Projekt Theater STUDIO, an intercultural experimental theatre in Vienna, Austria. Its new storefront space, FLEISCHEREI (BUTCHERIE), is a center for socio-theatrical performance with immigrants and other disadvantaged communities (e.g. cooking-shows with migrant artists or intercultural wedding-parties). She regularly directs in other Austrian theatres and has done design work in Basel, Switzerland and Berlin, Germany. She is also a founder of the Castillo Theatre, an experimental political theatre in New York City, which she introduced to the work of Heiner Müller. She earned her Ph.D. at New York University from the Department of Performance Studies under Richard Schechner. Her doctoral thesis, "HAMLETMACHINE Onstage: A Critical Analysis of Heiner Müller's Play in Production," (1994) remains a major touchstone for Müller scholars around the world.

Dan Friedman is dramaturg of the Castillo Theatre in New York City and editor of *Müller in America*, journal published by the Castillo. He has been active in political, experimental and community-based theatre since the late 1960s, when he was a member of the pioneering New York Street Theatre Caravan. He went on to help found Madison Theatre-in-the-Park in Madison, Wisconsin, and the Theatre Collective and Workers' Stage in New York City before helping to launch the Castillo Theatre in 1984. In addition to his dramaturgical and directing work with Castillo, Friedman has directed at La MaMa E.T.C., the Nuyorican Poets Cafe and at a number of New York City colleges. Friedman holds a doctorate in theatre history from the University of Wisconsin. He is the co-editor, with Bruce McConachie, of *Theatre for Working Class Audiences in the United States, 1830-1980* (1985) and editor of *Still on the Corner and Other Postmodern Political Plays by Fred Newman* (1998). He frequently writes about Castillo and other political theatre in both the scholarly and popular press, most recently in *The Drama Review, Modern Drama* and *Back Stage*.

David Kilpatrick is associate professor of Literature, Language and Communication at Mercy College. He earned his Ph.D. in comparative literature and M.A. in philosophy at Binghamton University, State University of New York. His current research focuses on the representation of violence in contemporary drama, and his writing has appeared in *The Brooklyn Rail, Theatre Journal, Journal of Dramatic Theory and Criticism, Didaskalia* and *Études Théâtrales*.

Aleksandar Sasha Lukac is a director and theatre scholar from Belgrade, former Yugoslavia. A graduate of Belgrade Theatre Academy, he has directed over fifty professional productions. Lukac has been artistic director at the National Theatre in Belgrade, Theatre Zoran Radmilovic and the independent political theatre, Plexus Boris Piljnjak, which was a catalyst of political controversy in Belgrade in the late 80's and early 90's. Lukac currently teaches at York University in Toronto and MacMaster University in Hamilton, and directs at Talk Is Free Theatre and Actors Rep Company. Lukac has recently guest directed three plays the Uzice National Theatre in Serbia.

Fred Newman was the artistic director of the Castillo Theatre in New York City from 1989 to 2005. He is the author of 25 plays and 8 musicals with Grammy award-nominated songwriter and composer Annie Roboff. An anthology of his plays, *Still on the Corner and Other Postmodern Political Plays by Fred Newman,* was published in 1998. He also directed the feature-length film, *Nothing Really Happens (Memories of Aging Strippers)*, based on his plays *The Store: One Block East of Jerome* and *Mr. Hirsch Died Yesterday*. Newman has frequently directed the work of Heiner Müller, including: *The Task, Hamletmachine, Explosion of a Memory/Description of a Picture*, and the American premiere of *Germania 3 Ghosts at Dead Man*, as well as two original theatre pieces featuring writings by and interviews with Müller entitled *An Obituary— Heiner Müller: A Man Without a Behind*, and *Mommsen's Future*. In addition, he has directed plays by Bertolt Brecht, Aimé Césaire, John and

Gabriel Fraire, Lawrence Holder, Yosef Mundy, and Peter Weiss. Newman is co-founder and principal trainer of the East Side Institute for Group and Short Term Psychotherapy. He is the founder of social therapy and has had a private psychotherapy practice for over thirty years. Newman has written five books on psychology, three with developmental psychologist Lois Holzman, that explore modernism and postmodernism, the theory and practice of social therapy, the politics of psychology, and the ongoing relationship between philosophy and social change. He received his Ph.D. in analytic philosophy and the foundations of mathematics from Stanford University.

David Robinson is a professor of English and Comparative Literature at Georgia Southern University. Though originally trained as a James Joyce scholar, his 1988 Fulbright in the German Democratic Republic led to an enduring interest in the living Brechtian tradition of German theatre. Dr. Robinson's books include: *No Man's Land: East German Drama After the Wall* (1995, edited); *Deconstructing East Germany: Christoph Hein's Literature of Dissent* (1999); and *Under Construction: Nine East German Lives* (2004, compiled, edited, and translated), a collection of interviews. He served for eight years as Secretary/Treasurer of the International Brecht Society. Currently he is doing research into computer-assisted learning assessment with funding from the National Science foundation.

Magda Romanska is an Assistant Professor and the Head of Theatre Studies at Emerson College's Department of Performing Arts. She holds a B.A. from Stanford University and a Ph.D. from Cornell University. From 2001 to 2002, she was an exchange scholar at the Yale School of Drama's Department of Dramaturgy and Dramatic Criticism, where she served on the editorial board of *Theater Magazine*. She also served on the editorial boards of *Palimpsest: Yale Literary and Arts Magazine, the Yale Journal of Law, Humanities* and *Diacritics*. Her recent articles have appeared in: *The Drama Review, Performance Research: A Journal of the Performing Arts* and *Women's Studies: An Interdisciplinary Journal*. Her book chapter "Hamlet, Masculinity and the Nineteenth Century Nationalism" recently appeared in an anthology published by the Cambridge Scholars Press. Her other contributions include: the *Encyclopedia of Modern Drama* (Columbia University Press), and *Theater Magazine*. She is the recipient of a Mellon Foundation Fellowship (2006), and is affiliated with the New York Council for the Humanities and the Literary Managers and

Dramaturgs of the Americas. She is also currently a research associate at Harvard University's Davis Center for Russian and Eurasian Studies.

Joanne Taylor is a Ph.D. candidate in Performance Studies at the University of California, Berkeley. Taylor's research interests include 20th Century acting and directing theories; Shakespeare in the 20th and 21st Centuries; editing theory; translation theory and performance; and Epic and Dialectical theaters. Her current project, "Time, Space, and Body: Locating Cinematic Performance," examines the cinema within a strictly performance studies paradigm in an effort to invigorate this popular entertainment form as a viable object of study for the discipline. Ms. Taylor has also translated and directed works by Brecht and Müller.

Carl Weber, who heads the Ph.D. directing program at Stanford University, is the major translator of Heiner Müller into English. He has published four volumes of Müller's plays, poems and prose in English. Weber began his career as an actor with the Heidelberg City Theater. In 1949, he was one of the founders of the Heidelberg Zimmertheater and directed the company's opening production. In 1952, he joined the Berliner Ensemble as an actor, dramaturg and assistant director to Bertolt Brecht, with whom he worked on the productions of *Katzgraben, Caucasian Chalk Circle*, and *Galileo*. After Brecht's death in 1956, Weber became one of company's directors, staging a revival of Brecht's *Mother Courage* production, scenes from *Fear and Misery in the Third Reich*, and, with Peter Palitzsch, *The Day of the Great Scholar Wu*. He also acted in eight Ensemble productions. Since 1961, he has directed for numerous theatres in Western Europe and the United States. In 1966 he was appointed Master Teacher of Directing and Acting at the newly founded New York University Tisch School of the Arts. He has been at Stanford since 1984. In addition to Müller, Weber has translated texts by Manfred Karge, Franz X. Kroetz, Klaus Pohl, Gerlind Reinshagen and Botho Strauss into English and his translations of English, French and Russian plays have been performed in Germany.

INDEX

15, 32
The Resistible Rise of Arturo Uri
(Brecht), 21
Revenge, 62, 64–65, 67–69, 94
Revising Germany (Newman), 3
Rituals, 137
The Road of Tanks (Müller), 40
Robinson, David W., 88, 89, 142
Romanska, Magda, 48, 49, 142
Romanticism, 27
Ronell, Avital, 79n12
Roy, Arundhati, 37
Russian Army, 27
Russian Revolution/Russian Civil
War, 41, 114-115

S
The Saint, 30
Satire, 27
The Scab (Müller), 14, 27, 40, 78n9,
93, 96
Scènes theâter cinéma, 3
Schneider, Michael, 123–124
Schwenkner, Inge, 14, 64, 77, 78n9
SCUM Manifesto (Solanas), 67, 68
SED. *See* Socialist Unity Party
Seeger, Pete, 48
Seghers, Anna, 41
Shakespeare, William, 29, 55, 65,
71, 77n3, 79n14, 136
Shakespeare and the German Spirit
(Gundolf), 62
Shakespeare Factory, 68
Sherbegia, Rade, 30–31
Showalter, Elaine, 71
Smithson, Harriet, 71, 72
Snatch, 30
Social Democrats, 13
Socialism, 27, 40
Socialist Realism, 109, 110, 118n4
Socialist Unity Party (SED), 13
Socialist Workers Party, 13
Solanas, Valerie, 67, 77, 78n10,
79n12
Soviet Union (U.S.S.R.), 20, 26, 40–
41, 106, 113, 118n4

Spartacist League, 36
Stahl, Hagen, 14
Stalin, Josef, 109, 113
"Stasi" (Ministry for State Security),
20
Stefanovski, Goran, 30
Steinweg, Reiner, 108
Stengel, Charles Dillon (Casey),
130–131, 139
Stiles, Diane, 3
Stramm, August, 23
Strittmatter, Erwin, 110, 118n5
Study of Hamlet (Conolly), 72
Surrey County Lunatic Asylum, 72
Suschke, Stephan, 2
Szeiler, Joseph, 1

T
The Task (Müller), 2, 3, 19, 35, 37,
40–42, 43–44, 112
Taylor, Joanne, 89, 143
Ten Days that Shook the World
(Müller), 14
Teraoka, Aileen, 53
Terrorism, 5
The Theater of Heiner Müller
(Kalb), 2
Theaters. *See* individual theatres
Theatre of Catastrophe, 121, 125-
127
Theatre Zoran Radmilovic, 24
"THEME OF A.S.," (Müller), 41
Thomson, George, 137
Tisch School of the Arts, 10
Tito, Josip Bronz, 13
Tracy, Ellen, 72
Trauerspiel, 52, 54, 55
Tristan and Isolde (Wagner), 21
Trotsky, 19

U
Utopianism, 109

V
Verfremdungseffekt (Alienation